"*My Intentional Life* will help you to identify 'Who-you-are-now' and 'Where-you-are-headed' as you establish an intentional culture in your life and home. Sheri explains how beliefs and values merge and determine the choices we make. She helps you identify what's working and what's not working in your life and gives you a road map to unclutter your life and live with purpose. A must read!!"

DR. BRENDA RAMBO
Psychologist/health service provider and author of
Understanding the Holy Spirit: Experience the Power

"*My Intentional Life* is a beautiful story with encouraging advice from an incredible woman whose heart is full of her love for God. It's one of those books I could read dozens of times, and get new inspiration each time about how to make my life more intentional every time I read it. Thank you, Sheri!"

BARBARA HEMPHILL
Author, Taming the Paper Tiger series

MY INTENTIONAL LIFE

*Connecting Your Heart
To Your Life and Home*

SHERI BERTOLINI

From Dust Publishing
Franklin, TN

From Dust Publishing, Franklin, Tennessee 37069
© 2012 From Dust Publishing
All rights reserved. Published 2009
Printed in the United States of America

ISBN: 978-0-9887798-0-8

Cover design by Chris Sandlin.

Illustration on page 10 by Sheri Smith Bertolini, 2012.

This book is dedicated to my husband, Roger,
and my stepdaughters, Elaine, Anne,
and Josclyn along with granddaughter, Sofia.

Remember, girls,
Bertolini women are smart, and strong,
and beautiful.

You have amazing hearts,
strength of character, and deep wisdom.
I am so grateful to be a part of your lives.

CONTENTS

FOREWORD

When I first heard that Sheri had gone into the business of organizing, I laughed. Not because the idea was ridiculous, but because it was so right. I was delighted. Organizing fits Sheri perfectly.

I first met Sheri when my family was preparing to travel extensively around the U.S. We needed a house sitter, and Sheri needed a house. The good news for Sheri was that while we were gone, she had room to roam. The bad news was that every time we returned home, Sheri's space shrank to a tiny bedroom/bathroom that had formerly been a side porch. But she made her accommodations work, fitting more belongings into that small space than I would ever have dreamed would fit. How did she do it? The O word. She was organized.

Organization does not come naturally to me. Fortunately, it comes second nature to Sheri. Over the years, she has organized our family office, video shoots, live concerts, travel, and perhaps the biggest challenge of all, our family basement.

But for Sheri, organizing goes deeper than just sorting and storing. Sheri sees household organization as the tip of an iceberg. What lies under the surface of our clutter is the real stuff of our lives. Sheri focuses first on life decisions. Who am I? Who do I want to be? What do I value? She walks us through what works for us and what doesn't in order to simplify the decision making that goes into getting organized.

So get ready to evaluate your needs, your desires, and your direction. Get ready to simplify and make room for who you really are and who you want to be, reflected in the space you create around you. Get ready to live your life with intention. You can have no more experienced guide than Sheri.

All the best!
Karyn Henley, award-winning, best-selling author

PREFACE

This is a book about your life. My life. All our lives. We all do okay—we move along, doing what we do. We work, play, daydream, nap, watch a movie, send an e-mail, mow the lawn, have a cup of coffee over the Sunday newspaper. We raise children, enjoy a meal with friends, get indignant when our intelligence is insulted. And we all wait for the next president.

This book is about what happens when you insert "intentional" into your life. Life can change dramatically when you add intention. This book takes a look at some, but certainly not all, of the factors, effects, challenges, and wonders of an intentional life.

The best any of us can do is say what we see from where we're standing. So if you can appreciate the perspective of a married-late-in-life, order-fanatic-turned-organizer, Christian-because-judgment-stinks-and-grace-works woman who loves to help people get "unstuck," then you may get something out of this book. Entrepreneur-author Seth Godin says, "If you can't say something with conviction, why say it?" If you're ready for change, you may find something here that inspires you to get unstuck.

If you're just curious, you might have a little fun. If you're a serious philosopher, you might be amused. You might even be challenged to think outside the box a little bit.

Here's to your life. Whether it's intentional or not.

ACKNOWLEDGEMENTS

Roger, I listen to you. Once again, you're right.

Nell, you're a great cheerleader.

Nancy, thank you for helping me see the big picture.

Lori, any editor who can keep me laughing through the learning curve deserves a medal. Or at least a vacation . . .

Also thanks to my army of editors, Tammy, Darcie, Peggy, Rénee, Rachel, Cheryl, Amy, Jackie, and Lynetta, for your detail-catching eyes and great edits.

Chris, you're a saint for the patience you offered me through the layout process.

Pastors John Sheasby and Mark Gungor, Dr. Brenda Rambo, Linda Spangle, Dave Ramsey, Seth Godin, Jon Acuff, Peter Lord, and John Eldredge—you've all played a key role in my journey. Thank you, and keep it up.

My immediate and extended family—the Smiths and Hauns— I am so blessed and grateful I grew up with all of you.

My centenarian Grandma, you are amazing. You have lived well and loved life. I'm so proud of you.

Thank you to my true and worthy Village People women: Nina, Blair, Nancy, Erin, Susan, Robin, Gloria, Cheryl, Kelli, Dawn, and Melissa. You rock.

"We are always getting ready to live but never living."

—Ralph Waldo Emerson

BECOMING INTENTIONAL

You know the saying, "Don't get your panties in a wad"? Well, mine used to be the size of a pistachio.

Growing up with conservative Christian values, I approached life with genuine faith and devotion to God. My efforts toward faithfulness and purity became labored with each reminder of my own failure. Frustration grew. My favorite consolation included another brownie and watching TV, trusting "Tomorrow is another day."

Signs of skewed belief started showing, peppering my twenties and thirties. I would coast along for a good period of time—months at a time—then something would trigger a meltdown.

It felt like I'd never measure up, never become this person I wanted to be, the person I thought I was supposed to be. God's blessing on me was dependent upon my performance, right? My best attempts were foiled. There was always something I could have, should have, done better. Failure, lurked and disappointment followed. But I kept trying.

As a single woman approaching forty, I found myself stomping up the stairs of my condo one afternoon, muttering and half praying, "Why can't I seem to pull my act together?" Midway up the staircase, a vision stopped me in my tracks. A clear image appeared in my mind's eye like a PowerPoint slide.

The picture was my tombstone.

In political cartoon style, my tombstone sat in tufts of grass. The rounded marble bore my name, though the last name was blurred, obscuring any sneak preview of my married name. The date of death was also cloudy. But the headstone's tribute was crystal clear. Instead of "Loving Mother" or "Faithful Friend" it said, "To Do List."

Two check box items were engraved below: "Live" and "Die."

"Die" was the only one checked off.

The tombstone's message hit hard—I wasn't living. My existence consisted of one "to do" list after another. Self-imposed rules and a steady stream of unrealistic standards had sucked the joy out of life. My satisfaction was wrapped so tightly around the impossible pursuit of perfection that failure was guaranteed.

Something had to change, though I wasn't sure how.

FASTING FROM FASTING

Not long after the tombstone experience, the pastor of my church announced a corporate fast. He invited everyone to fast for a total of twenty-one days. He instructed us to ask God what kind of fast each of us should offer. Some might abstain from food or a specific food, like desserts. Others might fast from TV or video games, and the really courageous souls would fast from complaining.

My autopilot setting selected fasting from food, as emotional eating continued to be a challenge for me. "And since it's only twenty-one days," I reasoned, "juices and water could be a good way to lose some weight in the process."

Day one came and went. I ended up eating something. Start over tomorrow. Day two, same story. Day three, all self-control caved in, and I found myself in the kitchen again. "This is ridiculous," I groaned. "I can't even fast right!"

God said, "That's because you're doing the wrong fast." Oops. I forgot. We were supposed to ask God what kind of fast we should do.

"I'm sorry, Lord, You're right. Okay, what kind of fast do You want me to do?"

God answered, "I want you to fast from fasting."

Pause. "Lord, I'm not sure I understand."

God explained. "Go out to eat. Spend time with friends. Shop and spend money on something you actually enjoy. Stop restricting yourself from everything. I want you to enjoy life and enjoy Me."

This was almost too much. I imagined a larger me and a smaller bank account. On the other hand, there were only eighteen days left in the fast; how much damage could I do?

Within three days of my fasting from fasting, coworkers asked if I was in love. Full makeup, snappy clothes, and sassy accessories reappeared from the bowels of my cabinets and closets. I experimented with a flat iron on my curly hair and produced a swingy new hairstyle. I was so happy I spontaneously hummed and sang while working. Dinner dates invaded my calendar, and decadent desserts inspired celebrations. I was having fun again.

My boss walked into the office during this fasting period, saw my new look, and said, "Girl, you keep this up and you're going to get a man." He was serious.

As it turns out, he was right. A few months later, I started dating Roger, whom I'd befriended a couple of years earlier. Now he is my best friend and husband. Our courtship is its own adventurous tale—but that's a different book!

The tombstone vision and the fast from fasting taught me a lesson that had a permanent impact: Life is a series of experiences to be enjoyed, not a checklist of tasks to be completed. After years of cranking out existence, dancing the do-everything-right-so-you-will-be-a-godly-woman dance, I was ready to sit this one out. I've learned . . .

- I wasn't living in purity; I was becoming sterile.

- I wasn't living a life of holiness; I was living in a vacuum without even tasting life.

- I wasn't becoming godly. My unique blend of genuine devotion with a large dose of piety left a bad taste in my mouth. My sincere pursuit of a godly life had gradually twisted into a noose. Failure, forgiveness, and raw, real life in all its glory and crazy messiness couldn't find room to breathe.

- Openings for true living were choked out by judgment of myself and others.

- I wasn't even living in reality anymore; I had created my own little world that depended upon rules, not God.

- I wasn't being real; I stuffed what I really thought for fear of being judgmental or sounding mean. My efforts to be nice and loving got mixed in with never really saying what I thought.

- I wasn't living in peace; I longed to know I was acceptable.

- I wasn't trusting God's acceptance of me. Instead, I depended more upon my own performance. The fear that God might remove His blessing from me was deeply real.

Roger was my living example of living life outside the box. He inspired easy conversation and could make anyone laugh. Total strangers would open up to him and talk about their lives. While I was cautious and tentative, he freely conversed with great versatility to both the shy teenager and the salty construction worker.

Roger's unconditional love and acceptance of me, whether I followed rules or not, provided me with the courage to test the waters of venturing from my safe box of rules. I discovered I enjoyed having a glass of wine with a normal dinner at home instead of only on special occasions. I learned I truly enjoy people. I liked spending a cool evening on the back porch with friends, playing cards, or just talking and laughing under the soft twinkle of Christmas lights hanging in the porch year-round. I even began to speak my mind instead of hiding my opinions, stuffing my feelings.

During our first years of marriage, my eyes opened wide. I had confined myself to a small box in the name of Christianity. My pinched view from inside the box didn't begin to make room for the breadth and depth of God's love. My scope of what was acceptable and appropriate left little room for the true me to be experienced by anyone. Neither could I fully appreciate others.

Embracing a larger version of God and His love for me introduced me to a larger scope of the world, allowing room for new experiences I would never have considered before. Such massive love provides coverage for all the fears and misconceptions that inspired me to hide in the first place.

This great quote by Erwin McManus sums up the way I had been living as a single woman for more than twenty years: "We have put so much emphasis on avoiding evil that we have become virtually blind to the endless opportunities for doing good. We have defined holiness through what we separate ourselves from, rather than what we give ourselves to. I am convinced that the great tragedy is not the sins that we commit, but the life that we fail to live."[1]

MASTERING DENSITY

Marrying at the age of forty-one earned me the title Miss "Someday My Prince Will Come." When I married Roger, I found myself moving for the twenty-first time, out of my two-bedroom condo and into a new life. This house included a wonderful screened-in porch, fireplace, and two of my three new stepdaughters, Anne and Elaine.

Two fully furnished homes with home offices, plus a music studio, collided. My life prior to marriage also provided me with a vast collection of souvenirs from my life as a single. So we now had wall-to-wall stuff in every room, plus the attic. And no garage. Our address could have been 220 Critical Mass.

During our first year of marriage, we designed a labyrinth through the front room among three desks, my music equipment, and several file cabinets. Turning sideways to get to my keyboard was exasperating. I couldn't find things I needed. Our house was confusing, not to mention hard to clean.

It was time to make a change. But instead of asking Roger or the girls to get rid of their stuff, I decided the purge needed to begin with me.

I commenced digging through everything that solely belonged to me from my closet, the attic, kitchen, laundry room, and front room. I threw together a three-day yard sale in one week. The only advertisements were colorful signs on our street. Almost a thousand dollars' worth of sales amassed just from selling old music equipment, duplicate kitchen appliances, and decorating items that no longer fit the house or my tastes.

Soon after, friends came over for dinner, and someone asked if we had painted or redecorated. Nothing had changed except the amount of stuff in our home. There was more space, more breathing room, and the atmosphere had changed. I was hooked. If one big yard sale of my stuff made this much difference, what else could be done?

SORTING IN THE ATTIC

I was inspired by shedding the first layer of goods, but it wasn't enough. I still had years of paperwork, keepsakes, and useless items crowding our living space. Returning to my boxes, I shoveled into the next layer.

Kneeling beside an open box in the attic, I found myself staring at mauve kitchen utensils. I wondered what ever possessed me to keep something so . . . so . . . mauve. It was laughable to see how dramatically my tastes had changed. I actually said aloud, "Wow. That's not even who I am anymore."

This may not seem like an epiphany to you, but for me it was one of those time-stands-still moments echoing through the attic. I heard myself make a statement out loud that was simultaneously brilliant and revelatory.

Suddenly, a new standard appeared—a golden measuring rod that could help me make decisions concerning all my possessions. My resolute Who-I-am-now materialized by simply identifying who I was not.

If I were a fairy godmother, this is the moment where I imagine myself gliding through the attic, touching each object with my What-Have-You-Done-for-Me-Lately? magic wand. Each item would give a little cry, sprout legs, and scurry into the donation box while I sang, "Bibbidi bobbidi SHOO!"

It was almost like magic. With new inspiration, I opened more boxes. The ease and speed of my decision making increased dramatically. Fresh perspective replaced dread. Bolstered by my new standard, I pried open each box of my history with anticipation. Every book, kitchen utensil, framed print, and backpack that declared, "I'm not who you are anymore," flew through the air, landing decisively in the donation box.

For weeks afterward, *Do you represent who I am now?* rolled over and over in my thoughts. This was not a matter for the attic alone. I was surrounded by artwork, clothing, and furniture from my past, each carrying a value that really no longer applied to my current or future life. Their season was over. They had served their time.

Embracing my wife and stepmom adventure launched me into a whole new world. My time, resources, decision making, and methods for making and keeping a home had all shifted along with my priorities for every aspect of my life. My values were different. Everything was different. So why was I still functioning with old paradigms and outdated materials?

Instead of me determining my new course, the circumstances of the day were leading me around by the nose. It never dawned on me I had the power to set the course and culture of my family and household. I was just trying to figure out how to make dinner out of canned tuna, leftover broccoli, and hamburger buns.

But even leftover broccoli was about to find its appropriate place as my Who-I-am-now led to my next discovery.

ME? AN ORGANIZER?

About a year after we got married, I started working part-time as an administrative assistant for a local banking investment firm. After about six months, I began to find the job less than satisfying. I thrived on detail, to be sure, but found the endless list of never-ending tasks discouraging. I could multitask with the best, but I also like a beginning, middle, and an end. I love the satisfaction of checking something off my list.

My creative nature grew flabby as I spent my time in tedium. Problem-solving amounted to "Do all the salutations in the database have periods or not?" Necessary? Yes. Inspiring? Not so much.

Tapping the keyboard of my computer one afternoon, I mused, "What do I do naturally, without even breathing hard, that would provide a service to other people, and I could make money doing it?" The answer came naturally: organizing. How simple. I stopped what I was doing and stared at the computer screen. Was it that simple? Could I create a business with my love for order and eye for detail?

I have never been able to talk on the phone without putting something away, leveling a picture on the wall, or straightening the fringe on the rug with my toe while chatting. In the greeting card store, I'm the one who puts the cards back in the proper slots with their mates if they have been misplaced.

I like countertops cleared, sinks emptied, clothes folded and hung. I am not a knickknack person. Simple, clean, and organized is my style.

Part of my compulsion for order is I honestly find it difficult to focus when there are lots of little things sitting about. If the walls are covered with pictures, the counters filled with baskets and papers and gadgets, and there are clothes draped over the back of furniture, it makes me crazy. I'm distracted by every little thing. Plus, I feel compelled to put it away because of my "work first, play later" upbringing. I am truly productive and have full focus when the area around me is clean and clear. It just helps me think and process.

Arriving at home after work that evening, I attacked the Internet to learn more about the professional organizing industry. I was not surprised to find thousands of organizers certified and specialized, writing books, creating products, improving homes and businesses. The attraction of running my own business increased.

I researched, devouring organizing books, talking to organizers, and building a platform from which to launch my own business. As I began working with my field-study friends, larger organizing principles took shape. It didn't take long to see that organizing was going to open the door to the heart and head issues of my customers. Having the skill to install effective systems was one thing. Handling emotional issues with high integrity, utmost confidentiality, and a deep level of trust was quite another.

People skills were going to be more vital than knowing how to alphabetize. But everything I'd been learning about God's acceptance of me was inspiring—I knew I wanted to pass it forward to my customers, caring about them without judgment.

I began in safe territory, offering free organizing to friends and family first, knowing they'd be nice to me! When those first three jobs went really well, I got brave and started putting the word out that I was starting an organizing business.

Immediately, my organizing jobs launched me into the world outside my protected Christian universe. I discovered new colors of beautiful diversity in people. As I worked with people of all faiths and lifestyles, enjoying entirely new topics of conversation, I learned about parts of life I'd never encountered. Their perspective in life became a gift to me as I helped them organize their treasures.

I particularly cherished the stories told by my elderly customers. The seniors with whom I've worked have the most amazing tales of life experiences. It is my honor to be a happy recipient of their telling. I gained a deeper compassion and appreciation for people of all ages, races, and beliefs. Strong friendships formed with those who would never have been allowed in my box before.

Through all these experiences, I began to see God was with me and for me. God had provided more for me than I'd given Him credit for. I was the one limiting myself and putting myself in the box. He didn't put me there. Neither did God give me a list entitled "The Things You Better Not Do or Else I'll Be Unhappy with You."

I became living proof that God didn't zap me with lightning, neither did He forsake me simply because I didn't follow my self-imposed rules. I used to be a proper priss. Now, sometimes I cuss. I used to go without basic needs just to make sure bills always got paid first. But now I spend money on me . . . and occasionally too much. Sometimes I don't put things away. I even went to bed without brushing my teeth once. You laugh?! I started finding out that failing didn't mean death. Failing meant I was fallible. I started embracing my imperfection, even though my heart's desire was to still try to achieve excellence and do the right thing. I created room for mistakes and gave myself permission to make them.

The biggest step I ever took was marrying Roger. I'd spent years devoted to waiting for "the right man." I had long lists of all his character traits and qualities. There would be no settling for second best, especially since I had waited until the age of forty and kept myself pure while I waited. Boy, this man was going to be something else! And he was.

I married a man who was not once divorced, but twice. He already had kids, and he was a baby Christian, and his finances were a mess. Gasp! (I say that with a smile now!) That's a big deal when you grow up believing there is a right and a wrong. It becomes law in your heart. Then, when you believe punishment follows wrongdoing, you live in fear—fear that you'll choose poorly and do the wrong thing. That's why it was so revelatory for me to learn that God doesn't fall off His throne when I fail.

I remember my sister coming to visit us after we'd been married for about a year or so. After a long conversation at the kitchen table, she just looked at me and said, "Wow, you've changed!" I had changed.

I changed from an uptight single girl eating brownies in her condo hideout to the wife of a crazy Italian with friends stopping by anytime for fellowship, encouragement, and a beer. Have all the fears disappeared? Not yet. Are all the rules gone? Almost. My error was being more devoted to rules and boundaries than to God's grace and gift of life.

God loves me. I believe it with all my heart. His love for me is not dependent upon my performance for Him. It is, instead, a gift I have received with deep gratitude. I will continue to shed the old rules and regulations. The taste of freedom on this side is sweet enough to keep me fighting for more. Everything has changed as a result.

WHERE WE'RE GOING

The level of personal freedom I have gained has directly impacted my life and my home. As I have organized in my own home and others', I've discovered that all kinds of organizing with all its related emotions, issues, and possessions can be navigated with the benefits of an intentional lifestyle. To succeed, you need awareness of your current identity, a vision for your life's direction, and tools to help you create a supportive culture in your home—all customized to fit you and your needs.

We will begin by building upon several basic principles to establish a common language. I'd like to introduce you to a journey with several scenic vistas along the way. Living an intentional life and establishing a culture in your home is a tremendously rewarding process. Occasionally, just as in any excursion, you may need an oil change or just want to take a breather at a rest area. Your car may even occasionally stall. But you will have opportunity to reconnect with the wonderful parts of you. You will gain better articulation of your current roles and goals. You may also discover new options for help and even eliminate some old issues that have bothered you for years.

You will have the opportunity to connect with your heart and gain a guide for establishing a culture in your home—an intentional lifestyle. All your possessions and surroundings can support Who-you-are-now and Where-you-are-headed. Your home can be a reflection of your unique expression of life.

I believe your home is not just a mere reflection of you; it is a living sculpture of you. A mirror's reflection is only a two-dimensional image. Your home is a supersized three-dimensional tour of your heart. But this sculpture is also functional. My goal is to help you create a home environment that serves as an inspiring launchpad to your day and a peaceful finish line at day's end.

And so begins our power walk to . . .

- identify Who-you-are-now,
- plot Where-you-are-headed,
- manage the challenges of change, and
- establish an intentional culture in your home, organizing accordingly

If you truly desire change, it means things will have to be different. If you are not happy with your way of doing things, it's time for a change. Living in the assumption you're on the right path is risky. Living in awareness that you're in a constant state of craziness is just as hazardous. But I believe the greater danger lies in knowing you need to examine your life but choosing not to. It all boils down to what's important to you and what you're prepared to do about it.

The first step is being willing to stop and question your life. Ask yourself these questions: Am I truly living? How do I know? When was the last time I checked?

Is your life accidental or intentional?

"Awareness without action
is worthless."

Phillip C. McGraw

"INTENTIONAL" MAKES A DIFFERENCE

"Intentional" changes the tone of whatever word it's describing. "Intentional" says somebody was deliberate. There was a plan, and it was carried out. It was preconceived, premeditated, plotted, schemed, designed, weighed, measured, or chewed on before it was executed.

Think about the impact of the phrase "accidental death." Now compare it to "intentional death." With the change of one word, we have a completely different tone and story.

Educational pursuits are intentional. Finding and keeping a job is intentional. Courtship is intentional. Moving your roommate's entire bedroom suite onto the front lawn for a great practical joke is intentional.

I love the stories of chance—accidental discoveries, unplanned inventions, and chance relationships. Such stories fill our history, portrayed in both film and literature. But I have a deep appreciation for the men and women, like George Washington Carver, Joan d'Arc and Florence Nightingale, who intentionally overcame adversity, pressing through the heat of personal and social resistance to achieve their visions. They impacted thousands. They lived intentional lives.

MEN OF HONOR, BLOWING THINGS UP

History resounds with honorable men and women of purpose and vision. Movies portray deeds of intentional kindness and courage. These aren't random acts. Intention fuels the difference achieved by each hero. My husband calls it "men of honor, blowing things up."

Roger doesn't use explosives, but he's still my hero. He intentionally makes the bed when I fly out the door for an early meeting. I intentionally look for interesting snacks so Elaine can have fun making her lunch. We intentionally invite people over for dinner, knowing the combination of personalities will provide hours of conversation and some great connections for new friendships.

Just because the scenario doesn't involve a burning building or a secret agent doesn't mean these acts are any less intentional, impactful, or heroic. Having an intentional life doesn't require an over-romanticized version of wide-eyed dreams at sunset or a slow-motion gaze over a cup of coffee.

So let's take a quick look at some familiar examples of intention. As you consider the various forms of intentional methods you encounter on a daily basis, you will more readily recognize intent in your life.

INTENTIONAL RETAIL STORES AND MARKETING

Think about what the shelves in a store look like. All the products are in tidy rows, labels facing front. The layout is intentional. At the checkout line, you are virtually surrounded by colorful, small items that transform into impulse purchases.

Think about stores where sale bins are filled with products all topsy-turvy. Unless you're the type who has the energy to dig for sale treasures, a lot of time and energy is saved with an intentional format in which all products can be clearly seen and accessed. I won't shop in certain retail stores due to their loose methods of display. I get completely overstimulated by the randomness of too many labels, colors, sizes, and categories. As a result, I go into an overload glaze and stagger back to my car.

I love stores with bright lighting, easy-to-find items, easy-to-read labels, and clear divisions of categories. I find I'm a much happier shopper as I go through the checkout line. I also have more energy to shop for longer periods of time. And they really buy my loyalty when their bathroom is spotless! Intentional attention to detail changes my entire shopping experience.

Think of your favorite stores, in which you shop frequently. You can probably sing their jingles, name the color(s) in their logos, and tell me what their employees typically wear as part of their uniforms. All of these elements are intentionally designed by the marketing genius behind each business. They have branded their culture, their look, their philosophy and mission, so you will easily recognize them. Every company employee follows specific guidelines to ensure a consistent experience of their culture and quality. They are rewarded for their efforts when you become a faithful customer.

WHAT DOES "INTENTIONAL" MEAN TO YOU?

I've given you some of my impressions of "intentional." Based on what we've covered thus far, decide which of the following activities reflect intention.

Stroll	↔	Power walk
Out for a drive	↔	Road trip
Doodling	↔	Painting a still life
Phone conversation	↔	Delivering a speech
Flipping TV channels	↔	Going to a movie
Telling a story	↔	Performing in a play

If you answered, "All of them," you're right. Some days you power walk because you need the benefit of the cardio workout or stress release. But sometimes you need to slow down and enjoy some time outside, so you stroll instead. Sometimes you need to have a conversation with someone on the phone, purely on a relationship level, just to blow off steam or talk about the funny thing that happened today. All of these activities are intentional.

To the general observer, one activity may seem to reflect a greater intensity than its more relaxed version. The natural assumption is the power walker is on a mission, whereas the person out for a stroll is taking it easy. To learn the true basis of their intent, you'd have to ask them. Don't assume you can spot intention from a distance. Even those messy bins in stores may be intentional if they believe you'll buy more, the more you dig!

Avoidance can be intentional. Denial and complacency can be intentional. Even living-by-the-seat-of-your-pants-because-you-don't-like-plans can be intentional. Judging an observed behavior or activity doesn't mean you can accurately pinpoint the intent behind it. Any act or absence of action can be deliberate.

INTENTIONAL LIVING: THE POWER OF CHOICE

A family pastor in California, Danny Silk, teaches Loving on Purpose, loosely based on the book *Parenting with Love and Logic*, written by Foster Cline and Jim Fay.[1] This brilliant approach to raising children instills the power of choice at an early age. His premise is that children need to learn how to make choices, even if it means offering the red cup or the blue cup. There isn't a wrong answer. Either cup choice is acceptable. Either way, the child gets a cup for his or her juice. The child learns how to exercise his or her individual preference and feel success through applying their power of choice.

While your children are young, you have parental authority to train their decision-making abilities, and still guide the outcome. For instance, one friend said she would bathe her daughter and say, "Do you want mommy to wet your hair, or do you want to do it?" Either way, the hair is getting wet, which is mom's goal. But the child participates in the process, learns decision making, and has opportunity for genuine input. Either answer is a good one.

Intentional living can produce any result you want. Choices are always available. First, you have to believe you have options. Then you choose to engage your will by acting on those options. Finally, you need awareness of possible outcomes and willingness to live with the consequences of your choice.

You can choose to live a life of empowerment, discipline, or engagement. You can live an intentional life of denial, medicating, or pretending. You may deliberately escape stress with a three-hour shopping spree, experiencing the elation of finding a deal, momentarily relieving stress. Maybe you go running for five miles to blow off steam. You grow tired of the yellow walls in your kitchen and decide to paint them blue instead. All choices result in different outcomes and consequences, and all of them are intentional.

Whether you eat a second helping of linguini, spend two hours helping a friend with his taxes, devour romance novels on vacation, or even purge the junk drawer when you feel stressed, you have, in fact, intentionally lived a few more hours of your life. Choices become a question of your intent—what do you want? Are you looking for an immediate result or a long-term goal? Some choices are healthier than others. Are you going to be further in debt at the end of "blowing off steam"? Are your choices doing damage or contributing to an improved life? You get to choose. And your choices vary based on Who-you-are-now.

Your definition of living inspires your choices. Our choices can easily be broken down into two categories: those that support life, and those that drain us of life. This may sound simplistic, but there is truth in the principle.

Having practiced a life of rules, I considered choices from the perspective of right and wrong. I believed one choice was the right decision, while the other options were wrong, leading to undesirable consequences. While this is true on some levels, I've found it much more fruitful to approach decision making from the standpoint of life and death. Does this option feed me or deplete me? The outcome will offer life or drain it away, according to my definition of true living. Consider the following choices I face on any given day:

- Get out of bed on time or sleep ten more minutes.
- Put the bill where it belongs or toss it on the counter for now.

- Eat the second helping of ice cream or put it away in the freezer.

These examples seem benign. They don't appear to carry the weight of life or death in their balance, do they? Small decisions that do not support your goals present the risk of undermining them. Over time, a string of small decisions makes the difference in reaching the goals or falling short. Your definition of life and death is represented in every choice you make, whether intentional or thoughtless. Remember, your approach to decision making is based upon your definition of living.

Some evenings, I put the ice cream away and am pleased with myself for using self-control. The decision produces life for me. Other days, I eat the ice cream because it is the perfect choice while sitting on the front porch, listening to the birds sing at dusk, enjoying memories of summers as a kid. When I choose to eat the entire half gallon of mint chocolate chip to soothe my angst, the end result is far from life-giving. I am disappointed and angry at myself. For hours, I wonder what possessed me to do something so detrimental—a life-draining result.

You may have heard the expression "death by inches." I am convinced of the inverse approach as well: life by inches. I suggest that you can gain ground in small decisions that produce life to you. When you continue to make small choices and decisions that add life to you each day, you begin to see positive changes. Now, when I eat the ice cream, I use a small ramekin, instead of eating directly from the carton. One small step for Sheri, one giant leap for self-control!

To determine if your life is leaking away, you must first settle on your definition of living. For me, true living means . . .

- becoming the best version of me
- living a fulfilling life, a life of contentment
- living out my passion—making a difference
- impacting the lives of others in a positive or beneficial manner
- knowing I have done my best to live my life according to my core belief and faith in God

When you develop your own definition of living, your launching pad for an intentional life is set. Becoming aware of your ability to choose is empowering. When you decide you are willing to engage in choice, you are ready for takeoff.

ARE YOU AWARE?

Living an intentional life means you are in touch with your life's big picture. As a result, you can hear the heartbeat of your purpose in your activities and choices. So the first question is, are you aware of your identity and your purpose? As a result, are you being deliberate or just reacting to what pops into your life? Or, as my friend Blair said, "Are you in an unexamined drift?"

When I took driver's education in ninth grade, we spent several class periods driving on the highway. In rural Kansas, two-lane highway driving was not exactly a hair-raising experience. Few drivers occupied the highway on a particular afternoon.

During my turn at the wheel, the instructor held his steno pad in front of the rearview mirror and asked, "Are there any cars behind you?" I didn't have a clue. I figured I had a fifty-fifty chance of answering correctly so I said, "No." He pulled his steno pad away from the mirror. Not one, but two vehicles followed close behind. I had focused so hard on keeping track of my speed and staying in my lane; I had no idea anyone had crept up behind me.

After that experience, I didn't have to be reminded to check my mirrors. "Unexamined drift" can prove deadly while driving. The same applies to day-to-day life.

Awareness is the result of frequent, consistent assessment. Checking your current identity and direction is a great idea, but it's also important not to obsess over every little change. For example, when trying to lose weight, how often should you step on the bathroom scales? Weighing multiple times a day is frustrating because your body weight fluctuates so often, providing different results every time you step on the scales. Most personal trainers or coaches advise you to only get on the scale once each week for an accurate representation of your weight-loss progress. Check in on a regular basis, maybe monthly or quarterly, and at most, weekly.

INSERTING INTENTION

People are, by nature, creatures of habit. Muscle memory and neurological paths are part of our makeup—we're hardwired for repetitive thought and physical responses. Our thinking—what we mull over and over in our minds—can become as routine as brushing our teeth before bed or your morning cup of coffee. Changing the course of our thoughts and challenging our beliefs requires exerting an act of will—a choice. We choose to interrupt the habitual routine and insert something new.

Think about how a woman experiences a monthly cycle, over and over. Until she's pregnant, the cycle doesn't stop. New life stops the cycle. If you find yourself circling the same mountain time and time again, making no progress, you will find the appearance of new life will end the pointless circling.

If you desire change, an intentional change, you have to stop long enough to assess your life. When you want to lose weight, assess what you're eating. When you want to save money, identify what you're spending. Stop the mesmerizing merry-go-round of routine. Unless you stop, and put pen to paper as a reality check, you risk remaining unchanged in a less-than-accurate reality. Your best opportunity for change is to stop the cycle long enough to be an investigator. Figure out what is really going on, and more important, why it's happening. Only then can you realistically determine how to intentionally insert change that will be effective and create lasting results.

In an honest assessment of your thoughts, the same process applies. You have to stop and look at what you think and why you think it. Identifying flaws in your way of thinking provides opportunity for change, replacing faulty beliefs with truth. Discovering your cherished beliefs provides clarity, reinforcing what is important to you. From this crossroads, you can choose to ignore your findings or live in awareness and explore new options for change.

Humankind's intentional decisions have produced everything around us from discoveries, to crime, to raising a family. In short, intention has contributed each horrible and wonderful part of life as we know it.

Let's look at the possibilities for great outcome using the three words of our goal—My Intentional Life.

MY INTENTIONAL LIFE

This time, it's personal; it's all about you. As you read this message, it's not about your children, your family, your friend, or your spouse. This is about you—your style, your tastes, your beliefs, your values, and the unique package of you-ness that stands apart from everyone else. This "my" includes your faults, flaws, and fears as well as your gifts, talents, pursuits, and achievements. When the airplane oxygen masks drop in front of you, you put on your mask first, then your child's. You need to be fully alive to provide life to your family. This is a time for you to get reconnected with the real you and revive your heart.

MY INTENTIONAL LIFE

Intentional life is a deliberate approach to life. Intent has to do with your forward motion, encompassing the way you make decisions, the way you behave, and habits you've adopted—whether they're deliberate or not. Intentional living includes getting (and staying) in touch with your core beliefs—the foundation of your attitudes, behaviors, and decisions.

MY INTENTIONAL LIFE

You may recall this quote from the movie *Braveheart*, spoken by the William Wallace character: "Every man dies. Not every man really lives."[2] True living is defined differently by each individual. You and I may not share the same ideals for what living means. The point of living an intentional life is taking the time to define your version of living.

A stark difference stands between existing and living. As you remember from the tombstone story in the first chapter, I'm inclined to live. I also believe we need reminders to check in and make sure we are truly living. Find your definition. If you have no definition of your own, gather ideas from those you admire, from resources you believe in. You may be able to articulate your own ideas after hearing others' definitions. Each one will vary. Define your customized version.

KEYS FOR AN INTENTIONAL LIFE

An intentional life is achieved using two factors. You've been introduced to Who-you-are-now. The second "W" factor is Where-you-are-headed. The combination of these two creates your vision for your life, which we'll designate as "V." In equation form, vision would look like this:

$$W_1 + W_2 = V$$

Who-you-are-now + Where-you-are-headed = Vision

If you are freaked out by math, hang in there. And for all the parents out there who said, "Yes, you'll use math later in life," you were right.

When you know Who-you-are-now and Where-you-are-headed, you have vision. Having vision is great. But having vision alone is a little bit like sitting in a parked car with a full tank of gas. You could sit in the driver's seat, key in hand, with a brand new GPS ready to guide you toward any destination of your choosing. You'll continue to sit in "park" until you make a decision—the final factor you need to complete your intentional life. Through our mathematic version, we now combine vision and decision together, resulting in an intentional life.

$$V + D = IL$$

Vision + Decision = Intentional Life

When you have vision, you are able to imagine and pursue what has not yet become reality. If you're a fully functional decision maker, you have the power to create forward motion toward your vision.

However, influences and circumstances of your life can squelch your imagination and vision. When that happens, life can seem hopeless. Perhaps you have identified a pattern of indecision in your life. Indecision operates like a choice—the choice to not decide. This choice can feel defeating, especially when you don't understand why you act the way you do. You have great ideas, but they just never seem to happen. You can feel stuck in mediocrity and chaos but want more out of life.

Having a clear, focused vision requires knowing Who-you-are-now and Where-you-are-headed. Decision making becomes the process of measuring everything against a standard—your standard. Once you define your vision, you can clearly see what fits or doesn't fit in your life—your "yes" and "no" get easier. You can own your life—the faults, the flaws, the wonder, the awes.

I believe people want their lives to count. They want to be remembered—to know their lives mattered and had value. What will they say about you at your end? Will you be remembered for an accidental or an intentional life?

It's all about you and what you choose. Having a clear picture and reviewing it often will help ensure you stay the course.

What kind of life do
you have now?

Are you present
and aware?

"Since you are like no other being ever created since the beginning of time, you are incomparable."

—Brenda Ueland

DETERMINING WORTH

As we build the foundation for creating an intentional life, it is essential to stir your awareness of worth. Without grasping the significance of your life, your possessions, even your values, it is difficult to create a framework for a deliberate, purposeful life. If you believe everything is worthless, you have nothing to lose.

Worth is an interesting concept. Perceived worth more accurately defines its meaning, for much like beauty, worth is in the eye of the beholder. We all assign varying degrees of worth to each part of life.

In the same way we have all agreed that paper currency with Abraham Lincoln's face is worth five dollars (remember, it's just a green piece of paper), we have also agreed a professional basketball player is worth more than an amateur. We have agreed that diamonds are worth more than glass beads. As a nation, we have agreed living in freedom is worth more than living under tyrannical rule. Cultures are centered around the agreements of perceived worth, be it physical objects, positions of power, or principles.

While organizing for clients, I've handled all kinds of interesting artifacts, art, and collectibles. I get caught a little off guard when the home owner proudly points out, "Hey, did you know that painting is worth about $10,000?" while I'm packing it for the upcoming move. My untrained eye never would have discerned such a high value for the painting. In fairness, you could visit my parents' house, see a skillfully painted duck decoy crafted by my father, and not have a clue as to its value either.

If I work for a client who collects dolls, we spend time discussing the dolls' worth. As she expresses each figure's value—market value or her own value—we can decide how to best store and display it. Do I personally assign worth to dolls? Yes, but purely as a sentimental value, as I have kept only a few favorites from my childhood. While working as an organizer, I temporarily adjust my "worth-o-meter" to the level of my client's. My job is to plug into her worth system and care about her treasures as much as or more than she does.

When you look at your home, do you see things you deem worthy? If you are not satisfied your home accurately represents what's important to you, how important is it to make a change?

How much is it worth to find papers when you need them, to clean your home quickly, or to invite guests over anytime? If you look around your home right now, you will probably see areas that carry greater worth than others—they are clean and orderly. When something's important to you, you find time to provide the care you believe it deserves. You make it worth your time.

WHAT'S IMPORTANT TO YOU?

Sometimes you really don't know what's important to you. Until you experience loss or damage, you may not realize how much you care. Let me give you a personal example.

I value my car. I know the resale value will increase if I keep up its maintenance and appearance. I must confess I get a kick out of buzzing around town in a clean, shiny car.

When I was single, I spent hours cleaning and detailing my Mazda 626LX. I used cotton swabs to clean out vents. I polished the tires and vacuumed and scrubbed the floor mats. Hand wax was applied once, if not twice, every summer.

During a holiday break, my cousin sat on the back end of my Mazda, then slid off to go in the house. As he did so, the rivets of his jean pockets gouged a long scratch across the trunk. I was livid. I was so angry, it even surprised me. I just stared at the long, deep scratch across my beautiful, burgundy, sporty, sun-roofed car.

Result? I don't let people sit on my car anymore. If they lean on it, I request they use care. The scratch experience taught me something I didn't know about myself. When others show disrespect for my belongings, it feels as if they don't value me. I've learned if something's important to me, I will find a way to get the results I desire most. Or I decide to not let it bother me. The choice is up to me.

Worth, simply stated, is your answer to two questions: Is it important to me? How important? The significance you apply to physical materials and intrinsic values becomes part of the framework that supports your intentional life.

The best part is, you choose. You choose to assign or not assign worth to everything in your life. Relationships, opportunities, shoes, and chocolate chips are all tagged with a degree of importance. You deem it worthy . . . or worthless. The object doesn't declare its importance. That power is in your hands.

FACTORS OF WORTH

Many years ago, I read a wonderful book by Peter Lord entitled *Soul Care*. The book presented principles of how to care for, understand, and manage a healthy soul. The author explored the question, "What is your soul worth?" and examined the premise that you are a soul, instead of possessing a soul.[1]

The part of the book that struck me most included several pages devoted to how we determine worth. Mr. Lord listed several factors, all contributing to our worth perception. The following headings are from Mr. Lord, while I've paraphrased the definitions.

WHO MADE IT?

Would you assign more worth to a house designed by yourself or a house designed by Frank Lloyd Wright? Why would one designer be more greatly valued over another? Who made you? Many would answer, "God." Some would say, "My parents," while others believe, "fate." The fact is you're here. Somehow, you got "made." Do you perceive thatyou are valuable because of who made you?

WHAT WAS MADE?

A little flute carved from a stick or a life-sized marble sculpture of a historical figure can evoke differing valuations of worth. At first glance, one object holds more perceived value than another simply because of what was made. Your frame of reference, your personal tastes, your belief system, and your life experiences all rush together, forming a valuation—the worth of the object that was made. Until you are persuaded differently, you remain content in your valuation.

UNIQUENESS AND SCARCITY

Which do you love more, the white diamond or the blue diamond? Do you find yourself irresistibly drawn to the original painting or the eleventh print in the series of one thousand? We are taught to believe rare, one-of-a-kind objects are to be revered. If it's "the only one left" or "the only one ever made" it's more valuable. Are you common or unique? Plentiful or scarce? I daresay there isn't another one of you running around out there, nor will there ever be. Uniqueness and scarcity increase worth.

PERSONAL PREFERENCE AND CHOICE

Value is the result simply because you like something. When you enjoy and prefer X over Z, you value X. What about you—do you feel preferred and chosen? This is a big deal. If you don't feel celebrated, appreciated, chosen, or preferred by someone, even yourself, you may struggle to feel valuable. But when you are cherished, you feel your sense of validation. You feel affirmed in the reason for your existence and valued for being alive.

POTENTIAL WORTH

People buy stock, gold, or real estate because it will hold or increase its value over time. An investor buys land because future development will make it more valuable. A collector buys a Star Wars toy on eBay because it will be worth more in fifty years.

Perceived value and worth are based upon potential growth. Do you have potential worth? What could you become? What might you accomplish in your lifetime? What legacies might you leave behind? The possibilities for the future are infinite. Remember you've already created a legacy with the life you've lived thus far. Your life has already impacted others and left a lasting deposit.

PERMANENCE

Wedding china is treated with great care while paper plates are tossed in the trash. Knowing an item will never exist again alters its perceived worth. Will you be around forever? You are not a disposable person with five more versions just like you waiting in the six-pack. As a Christian, I believe your spirit lives forever, even after your body dies. So you are, in that sense, a permanent being.

PRACTICALITY

When something works, and is found to be useful and helpful, productive and efficient, or just beautiful and pleasurable to experience, you deem it worthy. When something practical enriches your life, it is granted value. Are you practical? Are you functional to have around? Do you offer value as a helpful, engaging human to family, friends, and coworkers? The truly important question is whether or not you believe you are worthy.

If you see yourself filling a necessary void in the universe that can be filled by no one but you, you believe you have worth.

PRICE TAG

When I spend $150 for a pair of shoes, I'm going to take good care of those puppies. When I spend $2 on a pair of flip flops, I typically assign a more disposable attitude toward the footwear. They may last, they may not, but they'll probably fulfill their purpose for matching a specific outfit or two. But when I pay a high price, I offer more care to my purchase. I designate a higher level of worth.

What was paid for you? I don't mean what you earn per year. I mean, what has been paid for you? People have fed you, clothed you, cared for your physical and educational needs. People have put themselves on the line for you, given up their time and emotional energy for you. Even historically, valiant men and women have offered their lives as sacrifices for our protection and freedom. I believe God sent Jesus to die a sacrificial death for all individuals, paying for each of us to have abundant life here on earth, as well as eternal life with God after our deaths.

When anyone willingly lays down his life for another, the sacrifice is considered noble and valuable. There seems to be an innate sense of honor for "the last full measure of devotion"[2]— for the sacrificial offer of freely giving one's life for the sake of another—deserving or not—a high price indeed.

Think about the price paid for you and how it applies to your value.

How, then, do you assess the worth and significance you have assigned to yourself, your beliefs, your values? Often, until you experience loss, only then do you realize how much you care. But it's possible to identify your current values, understand their importance, and then position yourself to appropriately support their significance. Mr. Lord's list presents food for thought regarding our own perceived worth and that of the world around us. Now I'd like to add a factor of my own: learned worth.

LEARNED WORTH

When we grow from childhood into young adulthood, we are influenced by the values of those in authority over us as well as peers around us. We buy Ford vehicles because our dad always drove a Ford. We become Baptists because we grew up Baptist, as our parents and grandparents did. We wear Gap clothing because our best girlfriend swears it's the only thing to wear. Or we're Yankee fans because Dad hates the Red Sox.

Media and advertising wizards tantalize us with shiny images and alluring campaigns, convincing us their product is far more worthy than their competitors'. Sometimes we heartily believe them, investing in their product, becoming fans.

So let me ask you some questions:

- Why are you driving the car you're driving?
- Why do you live where you live?
- Why do you buy the brands you buy?

- Why do you believe your philosophies of life and/or religion?
- Why do you support your current cultural and political systems?
- Do you find yourself buying into the media propaganda or following another's example without really questioning why?

It's a good idea to take your own pulse at any stage of life and question yourself and your motives. Why are you assigning worth to the different areas of your life? You may be embracing a value that didn't originate with you, but was adopted from someone else instead. You adopted it long ago, and it no longer applies to you, but you've never taken the time to stop and look at it with a critical eye.

We are always in danger of becoming lulled by the routine, the mundane, and the autopilot setting in our daily lives. It's vital to question yourself on a regular basis: Why am I doing this? Why do I believe this? Why do I think this is so important?

Your worth is foundational to your entire belief system. As deep as that sounds, there is good news. You still have time to pursue this question and gain insight all along your journey. I am convinced we may never get a pat answer to the "Who am I?" But we can find out more as we grow and live, each new facet being revealed over time.

CELEBRATING YOU

I think birthdays are a big deal. When your birthday shows up on the calendar, it's time to fully appreciate why the day is celebrated. Your birthday is the day when a brand-new, never-been-seen-before person came into our world—and as far as we know, our universe.

This version of you will never appear again—not at this age, during this time in history, with the specific combination of beliefs, experiences, and gifts you possess. Brevity of life is certain; breadth of life is uncertain. You're here; you just don't know for how long.

We have the privilege of engaging with a wonder of life—you. We are honored to talk and laugh, work and play, hope and grieve with you. During your time in existence, we will hear your original thoughts and ideas and watch you tackle challenges in a way we would not have imagined. Your birthday is the day when all these experiences were made possible by your arrival on earth. I once heard it said, "You can only be fruitful where you are celebrated, not where you're tolerated." I agree. I choose to hang out with the people who celebrate me. And I celebrate them because I genuinely appreciate and value them. When we are valued, we become the best versions of ourselves.

If you are left with only one thought regarding worth, I hope it's this: You are unique, a one-of-a-kind, rare, never-to-be-seen-or-experienced-again life. And because of your sheer uniqueness, you have exceeding value. You offer an expression of life unlike any other, never to exist again. The world deserves to experience the full expression of you—uncut, unplugged, unashamed, and unafraid. You are worth the time, respect, and engagement of others.

What do you think you're worth?

"You have your identity when you find out, not what you can keep your mind on, but what you can't keep your mind off."

—A. R. Ammons

WHO-YOU-ARE-NOW

Are you the same person you were twenty years ago? Ten years ago? Five? Chances are, no. Is your family the same as it was five years ago? Two years ago? Even six months ago? Perhaps it seems to be the same, but a genuine look under the hood may reveal subtle differences. Those differences could prove helpful as you check your life's course. Life looks different than it did yesterday.

Living an intentional life requires the frequent asking of two questions:

- Who are you now?
- Where are you headed?

The first layer in our intentional life foundation is addressed in this chapter as we focus on the question, "Who are you now?" No matter who you are, one thing is certain. You are ever-changing, much like the circumstances and influences around your life.

Because change is constant, one of the first steps toward an intentional life is to increase awareness of your current status. You will need to take stock frequently. Keeping up with Who-I-am-now will provide a vital touchstone—a reference point—as you journey your life's path.

WHO AM I?

Volumes have been written about identity and the purpose for our existence. The answer to the "Who am I?" question is not a simple one. You are a complex being. A pat answer, like, "I'm a mother" or "I am a CPA" is not the answer you need for developing an intentional life. Your role is not your identity. It is part of the answer, but only a part.

We will look at many key factors. The total of all factors provides a more complete picture of who you are at any time. Uncovering "Who am I?" will be much more like releasing a combination lock than opening a padlock with a single key. In our quest to unlock Who-you-are-now, we'll take a quick look backward. Experiences from your life's history reveal themes and patterns that will give us clues toward your current identity.

Pretend you've selected choice photos from several stages of your life. In your mind, picture these photos in front of you, in any order. Or, if you need the physical experience, go grab a photo album and select some photos to examine. Choose a memory or a photograph of yourself from any of the following stages of life:

- under the age of ten
- during your teens
- during your twenties
- during your thirties
- during your forties
- during your fifties
- during your sixties
- as a newlywed
- as a new parent
- during retirement years

Think about what you were "into" during each of these time periods.

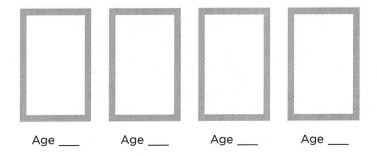

Age ___   Age ___   Age ___   Age ___

Now imagine a gift you would select for each past version of you. What would the perfect gift be? This gift can be material or intangible. Perhaps it is the gift of going out for coffee with a friend, or taking a nap.

The following is an example of me at four different ages and the gifts I would give to myself.

Age 7

TOY
DOCTOR KIT

Age 17

SONY
WALKMAN

Age 27

CAMERA

Age 37

MUSIC
SOFTWARE

As a kid, I loved animals, sports, crazy weather, and dessert. I still do. My love of medicine was born by the time I was in second grade, and I still love first aid, sports medicine, and physiology. The gifts I selected demonstrate how my interest in the creative arts soon overshadowed my pursuit of medicine during my late teens. A theme of creativity applies to my last photo. If I included a photo of me today, that same creative theme is still in the driver's seat.

Do themes from your past still exist today? Consider how some of your interests and values have changed, even though others have remained constant through the years. All these shifts through the years actively contribute to who you are today.

A dear friend of mine (the first editor of my manuscript) had a pen pal with whom she corresponded in second grade. The pen-pal relationship ended because Lori returned one too many letters with corrections included!

Another friend of mine has an adult son who is training in the culinary arts. She tells how when he was young, he was allowed to make his own snack one day. After what seemed to be a long period of time, she checked on her son's progress in the kitchen, only to find him placing his orange sections in a tiled, semicircle pattern on his little plate. Even as a little boy, food presentation was important to him.

Themes can appear at early ages. Aptitudes and talents emerge even while young personalities are still being formed. This pattern of early revelation does not apply to all individuals. Some children are easier to read than others. I know many adults who are still trying to figure out their purpose or talent in life.

Keep in mind Who-you-are-now is not limited to talent or aptitude alone. If this exercise was frustrating because you found no patterns or themes, do not be discouraged. We are only beginning to gather the first of many pieces of information about you. Once we round up a large array of samples, a more accurate picture of Who-you-are-now will emerge.

To conclude our exercise, add a current photo of yourself in your lineup. The perfect current gift for me would read, "Plane ticket." I want to visit my granddaughter, Sofia. Family is important to me, so I'm always scheming toward the next plane ticket and saving dollars toward that goal. Knowing who you are now, what gift would you give yourself today?

This exercise may have been revealing or just amusing. I smile to note how quickly my interest in dolls lost attraction. If you're reading this book, chances are you're no longer into dolls. Toy versions, that is. No matter what, it's good to just touch base with who you have been and how your experiences have brought you to Who-you-are-now.

Now that you've stretched your analytical muscles a bit with a mini-rerun of your life, I'd like you to notice something. Do you see how we used a few minutes to take stock? You always have the option of taking the remote control and hitting the "pause" button. Check in with yourself often. Are you noticing patterns? Have you noticed frequent appearances of behaviors or frustrations? Are you constantly returning to a dream list or saying things like, "Boy, I wish I could _____"? Pay attention. You're trying to tell yourself something. Are there adjustments you need to make? If so, keep those changes in mind as we continue take a closer look at who you are.

KNOWING WHO YOU ARE BY LEARNING WHO YOU'RE NOT

If you're not connecting with who you are, here is a great tool to keep handy: start with who you're not.

I recently settled into my organizing identity after experiencing who I'm not as an organizer. I faced the decision of specializing in office filing systems or continuing with residential organizing. I decided to give office work a try. After weeks of training and developing a new website, logo, procedures, and printed materials (and spending several hundred dollars in the process), I started to figure out I was not cut out to be an office filing person. I didn't enjoy it. I still don't. I can do it, but I find it draining.

I tried to convince myself I'd be great. Office organizing beckoned with its allure of more money in less time. I imagined myself performing organizing miracles, increasing office productivity, earning the praise of the corporate world. Visions of me in a crisp power suit and CEOs handing over large checks with grateful smiles made me feel strong and influential.

But several weeks into the training, I still wasn't making phone calls to businesses. I did anything to avoid it. I'd sooner create another brochure than cold-call a business. Far more time was invested in composing lists of people to call than in actually calling.

I finally had a "come to Jesus" meeting with myself and asked some hard questions:

- Why aren't you pursuing this?
- What are you afraid of?
- How is office-system work a good match for me?
- How do I perceive this is a poor fit for me?
- What did I think it was going to look like?
- What does it look like in reality?
- What do I want to do about it?
- Can I take a loss and still survive? (Financially, emotionally, if I fail, etc.)

My conclusion was no, I honestly wasn't enjoying this pursuit. Office organizing didn't inspire me to leap out of bed. My passion is organizing with individuals in their homes. It's personal, nonthreatening, and the results are so satisfying. I often see lives changed through organizing a home, and I get totally jazzed from the results. Office work didn't offer me the same reward.

Becoming an office organizer was costing me more than I was willing to pay. My peace of mind was shot. Creative energy drained away, replaced by dread. I value my emotional and mental peace too much to sacrifice it for making more money—especially doing work I don't enjoy. I'm not afraid of hard work, but my efforts didn't connect with my heart.

So I resigned my position in the training. Was the training good? Absolutely. I learned a great deal. Several tools and methods were added to my organizing arsenal as a result. I also overcame personal obstacles that prevented success in my own paperwork and filing. Home offices, which I previously avoided like scary movies, are no longer daunting to me.

I learned who I'm not, which was worth the price of admission. Just like trying on a bikini in front of a three-way mirror under fluorescent lighting—it just wasn't working. Granted, I could lose more pounds, get a tan, body build, and improve my physique. But frankly, I'm just not invested enough to commit the discipline, the hours, the money, and the effort it would require to look great in a bikini. It's not a good fit for me and it's not important enough to pay the price.

So I remain a residential organizer. And a one-piece swimsuit gal.

Be encouraged by narrowing the field. Take a moment to list some of the things you know you are not. Give yourself permission to express frustration or perceived failure. It's quite freeing to admit there are some things you aren't and never will be, nor do you ever desire to be. I've included a couple of examples to help get you started.

WHAT I AM NOT . . .

- I'm not a perfect parent.
- I'm not a perfect housekeeper.
- I will never be wrinkle-free again.
- I'll never be like so-and-so . . . I'm me.

See? Even in this short list, I end up stating what I am. A sense of resolve is stirred in the process of stating what you're not and never will be. When you reconnect with your heart, the revelation can be quite satisfying.

FULLY YOU OR EMPTY SHELL?

Identifying who you're not is almost as important as knowing who you are. Both contribute to your ability to be fully you. When you are uncertain of your strengths and weaknesses, your identity can feel half-baked, lacking confidence. When meeting someone for the first time, you can tell immediately if that person is confident or apologetic about who he or she is. It breaks my heart to see those who've squeezed themselves into a mold of someone else's design. Meeting a real individual is a remarkable encounter.

When I visit a foreign country, I experience sights, sounds, smells, tastes, and a mind-bending stretch of customs and ways of thinking different from my own. Much in the same way, I long to experience each person I meet. Each personality is a never-to-be-seen-or-experienced-again version of life. I want to relish the experience and see his or her precious value.

Identical twins have different identities because they process their world differently. They can be fed the same circumstances, information, and even sensory experiences. Yet they can internalize their data in completely different ways, resulting in a frame of reference worlds apart from their mirror duplicate. Each twin holds a unique offering—each can be experienced as a complete individual with all the complex facets of emotional, spiritual, and psychological makeup. Each of them is an individual identity.

Let's look at short passage of scripture for a moment. First Corinthians 13 gets a lot of attention at weddings and is even known as the Love Chapter. It offers what I believe is the best description of the nature of love. My husband and I adopted this passage as a standard against which we measure our beliefs, principles, and values. We printed out the passage, displaying it on the front of our fridge. When I suspect I've been out of line with something I've said, or if I'm toting a bad attitude, I'll often turn to this passage and check myself against this love-o-meter.

The following excerpt addresses our lack when we do not have love:

I CORINTHIANS 13:1-3

If I speak in the tongues of men and of angels, but have not love, I am only a resounding gong or a clanging cymbal.

If I have the gift of prophecy and can fathom all mysteries and all knowledge, and if I have a faith that can move mountains, but have not love, I am nothing.

If I give all I possess to the poor and surrender my body to the flames, but have not love, I gain nothing.

The author of this passage created a great metaphor of our existence as empty shells when our actions are shallow because we do not have love as our driving force. Much in the same way, when we live our lives in survival mode, wringing every cent from every paycheck, allowing circumstances to push us around; we are in danger of becoming shells of the true version of ourselves. If we are grounded, solid, and truly know who we are, life's winds can push, but we tell them which way we prefer them to blow!

Before I became more grounded in my Who-I-am-now existence, I was blown about by a slight breeze. My boundaries were almost nonexistent. I had little confidence in myself and spent a good portion of life hiding away, consoling myself with brownies. I was frustrated with both my lack of confidence and my brownie dependence. I was much like an empty shell with occasional appearances of the true Sheri.

I used to depend on my musical abilities as a worship leader and composer as my identity. My faith was a weird mix of true faith and religious performance. I was driven by frustration, fear, and worry. My operating mode was set on "Uptight" or "Unhappy," resulting in a lot of hiding from social settings unless I felt comfortable with safe friends.

Now, I strike up conversations with strangers. It's not always comfortable, but I don't hide like I used to. My faith is more genuine, without the exhausting, religious rules and regulations squeezing life out of me. Freedom to express myself has dramatically increased, and I seek others out, encouraging them. I am truly enjoying who I am.

How did I arrive at the place where I enjoy who I am? It took years of uncovering faulty beliefs, exposing lies I had believed about myself, others, God, and life in general. Close friends and family walked with me through a labyrinth of change. My husband was, and continues to be, my biggest influence in helping me shed old baggage. I'm learning to be real. I'm no longer dancing to others' tune, others' expectations and rules. I have chosen for myself. I've learned I am an interesting person with all my salt and vinegar, sweet and sour. No more apologies for being different or disagreeing. How freeing.

If you have spent any time watching home makeover shows on television, you know they are quite inspiring. As an organizer, these dramatic transformations can also set up clients for unrealistic expectations for the quick fix they hope to see in their own home. I explain to my organizing customers that progress may seem slow during the initial stages of work, but there will be a day much like the big "reveal" moment highlighted on the TV shows. Sure enough, the day arrives when the room is absolutely transformed, with everything in its place, and the client is thrilled.

Unrealistic expectations can also discourage you as you attempt to define your identity. Oh, wouldn't it be great if we could yell "Move that bus!" and our identity would be standing there, gleaming, like an extreme home makeover.

Uncovering your true identity takes time and investigation, more like a treasure hunt—and the treasure hunt continues over a lifetime as you change and grow. When attempting to define something as complex and ever-changing as Who-I-am-now, it helps a great deal to break down your identity into some basic components. The Clouds of Influence diagram in our next chapter will help you articulate some of these elements contributing to the current version of you.

How does your identity
differ now?

_____

How is it the same?

_____

Are you okay with that?

"The more you know who you are and what it is that you want, the less things bother you."

—Bob Harris in *Lost in Translation*[1]

THE CLOUDS OF INFLUENCE

I am a visual learner, so diagrams are helpful when I'm learning a new concept. One afternoon, I sketched out a cloud diagram in an effort to explain to my husband what I'd been writing about.

In the diagram, you are at the center, surrounded by five Clouds of Influence: Roles, Dreams/Goals/Passions, Feelings, Beliefs, and Values. Each day, you are impacted by the power of any combination of clouds. Much like changing weather, these clouds constantly shift in weight and intensity. As these influencers shift, changes are produced in you. The nature of Who-I-am-now can be affected in a single moment. Let's look at each cloud, how it behaves, and how it impacts you.

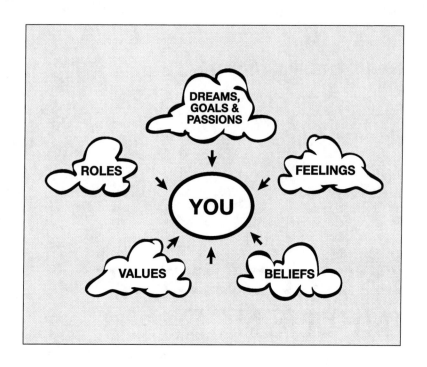

CLOUD FORMATIONS

The bottom two clouds, Values and Beliefs, are positioned to represent the foundational nature of their influence. What you believe and value—what you think is true and important—offers great bearing to your stability and direction. Behaving much like foundational footing, this pair contains your core set of standards, your morals, ethics, and ideals. These principles are not as likely to change over long periods of time. They can change; it's just not as likely.

The clouds to the right and left, Roles and Feelings, are much more fickle by nature. Their behavior is more fluid and unpredictable. Just like weather, they can change in a moment, ranging from a slight drop in pressure to a full-blown thunderstorm. In the same way that Beliefs and Values grow and deepen over time, the slightest breeze of change in the air can cause reactions in the remaining threesome. If you are not fond of change, these clouds are not your best friends.

Roles and Feelings clouds act much like a train engines. Have you noticed how an engine moves a train whether positioned at the head or the tail? Roles and Feelings have been placed at the right and left in the diagram to depict their service as powerful forces, pulling and pushing you through your day. Sometimes they're train stoppers!

The Dreams/Goals/Passions cloud is positioned overhead to remind you that you're reaching for something higher. The goals you pursue are just beyond where you are now, inspiring you to move toward your dream.

Each person's cloud definition will differ. What looks like a goal in my cloud may be a role in someone else's cloud. My definition of feelings may contrast greatly from my sister's. Your most important value may be one of my pet peeves! Intentional life is built upon the premise of you defining your life, not someone else's. The inverse is also true—don't let others define your life.

Let's look at some of the specific elements that shape you, and provide some language to express Who-you-are-now. We will begin with the five Clouds of Influence, providing an overview and definition for each. All the clouds impact the way you define yourself and your home.

ROLES CLOUD:
WHAT I AM AND WHAT I DO

Your days are filled with roles and titles. The number of roles you fill has great bearing on how you spend yourself. Answering the question "Who am I?" is daunting. Answering "What do you do?" is much easier to articulate.

To provide perspective on how your roles influence you, we are going to separate the parts you play from your identity. You are _____ (fill in name here). You wear roles, much like hats. You are not a hat; you are so-and-so (see name above). Wearing hats reflects purpose in your life. You may be wearing hats that no longer fit or are sorely outdated. Some hats may have been jammed onto your head when you never wanted them in the first place. And in many cases, you're wearing so many hats at once, it's hard to keep them from falling off.

When your roles are clearly identified, you can see how they shift and grow in importance, creating different needs for you and your home. Let's look at how your Roles cloud works.

Envision a working mom. Let's say she's a teacher. All it takes is one phone call and now the role of Mommy-the-Nurse kicks into gear because her son has a fever. Another role is added to Mom, and her day changes. She gets a substitute teacher to cover her class and leaves work to care for her sick child.

Mom's Roles cloud expanded with the addition of Mom-the-Nurse. But once her child recovers and returns to school, Mom goes back to her original Role combination. It can look something like this:

MOM, WIFE, TEACHER

▼

Care for sick child at home, missing work

▼

MOM, NURSE, WIFE, TEACHER

▼

Child recovers, goes back to school

▼

MOM, WIFE, TEACHER

Note what happens to the role of Teacher in the above diagram. See how the role started one size, diminished, then returned to its original size? Think of a role you've had to temporarily put on a back burner. Does it mean you've given up, or a part of you has disappeared? Not necessarily, though it can feel that way.

In the same way the words in our diagram expand and contract, Mom's Value and Feelings clouds may also increase as the importance of her child's well-being expands. While her child has a fever, her value for health is amplified, even if only for a couple of days. She may also experience the emotions of frustration or heightened concern.

When the child recovers and goes back to school, Mom returns to her work and her Role, Value, and Feelings clouds relax to their previous size—unless the experience created a permanent change.

What if this is the sixth time this year the same child has missed school for the exact same symptoms? Inexplicable illness is frustrating, even alarming. Mom's Values cloud could shift permanently. She may devote time to research, looking for answers and the source of her child's condition. Sickness prevention becomes her Dream/Goal/Passion. These alterations in the mother's clouds of influence may remain as long-term changes, possibly altering her course forward on her timeline.

Roles play an important part in Who-you-are-now. The more demanding the role, the more intense its influence. Intentional awareness of the roles you play provides understanding of their influence on your identity. Recognizing your roles offers a sense of security and direction so decisions can be measured in light of the titles you currently wear.

DREAMS/GOALS/PASSIONS CLOUD: WHAT I WANT

Dreams are a strange paradox. Some dreams are so strong they keep us alive, helping us survive formidable circumstances. Dreams can also seem delicate and fragile, easily crushed and bruised by others' criticism, disappointment, or disbelief.

You may wonder why Dreams, Goals, and Passions are grouped together as one Influence cloud in our diagram. This trio could easily be broken down into their different definitions.

For our purposes, however, I am more interested in presenting them as motivators. All three factors offer you a source of power to drive you forward, providing inspiration to keep you moving. All three are effective energizers. Staying plugged into your motivators keeps you feeling hopeful and moving forward.

As a child, I heard orchestras in my head. A constant stream of melody, instruments, or singsong patterns played in my mind— tunes only I could hear. Early on, I also showed an aptitude for music, easily singing melody and harmony.

Thirty years later, when technology had advanced enough, I was finally able to take the orchestra from my head and play it into computer software through my piano keyboard, so others could finally hear what I'd been hearing since childhood.

From the moment I listened to my first orchestration, I wanted to produce my own CD. It took the next five years of composing, arranging, and learning how to produce a CD before it all came together. Finally, my first CD was born.

The winds against me? I waited for more than thirty years for the technology. It took several years to finish composing and arranging. Mixing and manufacturing took weeks. But it happened. I kept plowing. The learning curve wasn't blissful, but there was joy in the ride because my Dreams cloud kept me moving forward.

We can all draw inspiration from others as examples of fighting for our dreams. But they are just examples. It is up to us to fight for what we believe is important. If your Dreams cloud is important, you will continue to push against the prevailing winds.

FEELINGS CLOUD: WHAT I FEEL (PHYSICAL, EMOTIONAL, SPIRITUAL)

Some scoff and say what you feel holds no bearing. I beg to differ. Others say being controlled by your feelings is dangerous or reckless. I agree. I also understand how feelings can be misleading when you lack maturity and discernment. Allowing pure emotion to drive you is dangerous. On the other end of the spectrum, some people are so out of touch with their feelings, they no longer connect with what they enjoy or desire. In both extremes and in all levels between, feelings are influential in how you approach life.

We need our feelings. They tell us, "This is a big deal." When you hear yourself say, "That's just not as important to me as it used to be," you are reading a shift in your values through your feelings. Pay attention. Your feelings indicate changes in Who-you-are-now.

Your Feelings cloud can rock your world with its shifts and expansions. The shock of losing a loved one can render you almost nonfunctional for a period of time. Stress resulting from failing finances or work-related tension can manifest in physical symptoms, like increased blood pressure, change of appetite, loss of sleep, and heart palpitations. Extreme emotional upheaval can slow one's life to a level of survival and existence instead of a fulfilling, fruitful life.

On the flip side, someone who is in love or just became engaged can be deliriously happy. The inspiration of the promotion, the freshly acquired master's degree, or the positive pregnancy test lights up the Dreams cloud. A new job, a new friend, a loss of thirty pounds can heighten confidence and bolster your motivation. Good news and happy times provide great fuel to speed you along your way.

BELIEFS CLOUD: WHAT'S NONNEGOTIABLE?

You have beliefs about all aspects of life. Everything you understand as truth exists in your makeup because you decided to believe it is true. When you are introduced to new information, you process it, determine whether you agree or disagree, then embrace which parts you decide to be true. This process can be applied to tasting a new dish or deciding if you believe in God. You assess, weigh and measure, embrace or reject. All the parts you embrace become part of your core belief system.

Your beliefs are fundamental to your identity and encompass more than your spiritual faith. Every experience in life offers opportunity to draw conclusions. Your parents, mentors, and teachers deposited beliefs in you, but you developed your own independence. As you grew into young adulthood, you began to measure the validity of these inherited beliefs, then either embraced or rejected them.

Some beliefs are adopted based primarily on your experiences. After suffering years of academic struggle, you may conclude you're not a good student. Years later, you could be diagnosed with dyslexia and learn you are quite intelligent; you just need to utilize new methods to absorb information. Now, instead of dreading school and believing yourself to be unintelligent, your belief shifts and your life's course is altered as a result.

Let's say you go out for a pleasant stroll on a sunny afternoon. As you walk, you notice a large dog approaching. Just one moment ago, you were operating under the belief of "I am enjoying my walk. I am safe." You felt safe because you believed it was true.

In a single moment, all of your doggie belief systems come rushing forward. If you believe "Dogs are great; I love dogs," then you're happy to see him. However, if you believe, "My brother was hurt by a dog; I might get hurt," you experience an adrenaline rush. Either dog-belief collides with your pleasant stroll belief, producing what happens next. You might do any one of these things:

- stop walking, bend down on one knee, and extend a hand, saying "Come here, boy!"
- lunge suddenly at the dog, shouting, waving your arms, hoping to startle the animal into submission and flight
- pray, "Oh God, oh God, oh God, make him go away, make him go away, make him go away," while breaking into a run

In each case, a belief produces an outcome. What you believe evokes your response and creates the end of the story.

Consider what you fight for, argue for, support, and defend with your finances and time. Think about the issues you vote for and write to your congressman about—these are some of your deep beliefs. When you find yourself awake in the middle of the night, praying, you own a deep-seated conviction. The intensity of your belief is revealed when someone else treads upon it.

Even subtle beliefs are part of who you are. If you subconsciously believe you don't really deserve nice things, your shopping habits will differ from that of someone who believes she's a princess. If you believe play comes after work, you will plan your time around the assurance that all work is complete before you sit down and relax. Beliefs and values merge and weave tightly together at times. For the purposes of this book, you only need to focus on the combined power of your beliefs and values that merge into your unique guiding force through life.

VALUES CLOUD: WHAT'S IMPORTANT TO YOU?

A value could simply be defined as an essential quality you have deemed as good, worthy, and helpful. As you grow and mature, your values can change. Your likes, dislikes, and beliefs may also change. The life you have experienced up to this moment has shaped your frame of reference, which is then applied to all aspects of your life. Your experiences have served as an interesting educator.

When you walk through an experience, you reevaluate your values based on what you just encountered. A circumstance will either challenge or confirm what you already believe. If you decide to replace an old belief, you modify your values. If your family's health improves due to dietary modifications, you are likely to reassign a higher value to healthy eating. This change can potentially influence where you dine and shop for groceries. Some experiences reinforce what you already valued or believed, thereby deepening your resolve.

If you've experienced identity theft, it's possible you will reassign a greater value to protecting your personal information, increase the strength of your computer firewall, and add stringent parameters to your children's computer use. If you believe parking in the far end of the parking lot avoids dings in your car door, you will continue the pattern as long as your parking experience proves you're right.

Values shape you. Experiences mold you. And the choices you make determine your life's course. In the movie, *Renaissance Man*, Danny DeVito tells his students, "The choices we make dictate the life we lead."[2] Our choices continually shape our lives. We make conclusions based on the experience of our choices. Our experience then forms our beliefs. Our beliefs and values merge and determine the choices we make. The circle continues as we age and grow.

As we mature, different ages bring changes. We go through school and start careers, we change careers, and we change addresses. We see the arrival of our grandchildren and draw closer to retirement. We welcome new friends and grieve the loss of old. During all these transitions, some of our values alter, while other core values strengthen and do not change.

FEELINGS, BELIEFS, AND VALUES TABLE

Here is a travel-sized list of words that can all be considered feelings, beliefs, and/or values. These words are meant to provide a springboard to help you articulate what is currently important to you. Feel free to circle or highlight the words with which you feel a strong connection or appreciation.

FEELINGS, BELIEFS, AND VALUES TABLE

Abundance	Exploration	Focus	Happiness
Diligence	Intelligence	Modesty	Perseverance
Realism	Sexuality	Structure	Truth
Acceptance	Ambition	Capability	Courage
Diversity	Fairness	Freedom	Harmony
Imagination	Justice	Optimism	Power
Relaxation	Simplicity	Support	Uniqueness
Accuracy	Appreciation	Charity	Courtesy
Education	Faith	Fun	Health
Impact	Kindness	Order	Practicality
Resourcefulness	Spirituality	Synergy	Usefulness
Achievement	Assertiveness	Commitment	Creativity
Efficiency	Family	Generosity	Honesty
Impartiality	Leadership	Originality	Privacy
Reverence	Spontaneity	Thriftiness	Vision
Adaptability	Attentiveness	Compassion	Curiosity
Entertainment	Fearlessness	Gratitude	Honor
Ingenuity	Love	Passion	Prosperity
Security	Stability	Traditionalism	Willingness
Adventure	Balance	Confidence	Daring
Excellence	Fitness	Growth	Hospitality
Integrity	Loyalty	Peace	Punctuality
Sensitivity	Strength	Trust	Wisdom
Affluence	Beauty	Contribution	

Now that you've warmed up your brain toward the concept of feelings, beliefs, and values, I need to expand the definition of values for the purposes of this book.

You may have looked at the word list and thought, "But that value is one of my beliefs" and you're exactly right. A value for one person can be considered a belief by another. Yet another reader could look at these same entries and say, "But those are feelings, not values." Exactly.

The point of an intentional life is for you to be in touch with what these words mean to you. You interpret things uniquely. Your filter system is one-of-a-kind because of your history, influences, and frame of reference. Your education also impacts the way you articulate feelings, values, and beliefs. All of these elements affect and cross-pollinate each other. So I cannot define your values for you. Neither can anyone else.

You are in the process of intentionally taking stock and identifying what is important to you—what resonates in you. This is about how you connect with the rhythm of your heart and then let it pulse through your life and home.

When you look at the list above, you may see qualities vital to you. When you feel strongly about a principle and it has not changed during your lifetime, you are most likely looking at one of your beliefs.

Your family history can begin to make more sense as you identify consistent traits through your personal history. Looking at your siblings and parents, you may find reasons you share or reject particular feelings, values, or beliefs with other family members. This may help you understand what makes you tick and might also raise some interesting questions you'll wish to explore further.

For the purposes of developing an intentional life, we will include several elements under the heading of Values. Likes, dislikes, favorites, pet peeves, styles, tastes, and current trends will all fall under this heading. Values, for our purposes, will include anything currently important to you, apart from your nonnegotiable core beliefs.

HOW IMPORTANT ARE YOUR VALUES?

As you explore your values, you discover different levels of importance you've assigned to each one. You operate out of values you hold dear, values you never really thought about. Consciously or subconsciously, you have ranked your values in any of the following classes:

- sort of important
- a pretty big deal
- you can take it from me when you pry it from my cold, dead hands

Each value carries significance. You quickly discover the importance of your values when two of them collide and you are forced to choose one over the other. Have you ever flipped a coin to decide between two choices? Sometimes when the coin lands, revealing you have to go with the tails option, only then do you realize you really wanted heads. Your feelings are the temperature indicator of your heart.

If you like something, the way it tastes, the way it fits or looks, it is a value. If you have an appreciation for a retro style or love of natural wood, each receives an invisible stamp in your mind that says: IMPORTANT. When you assign importance to a value, you seek it out and make room for it in your life. Your taste in fashion, music, furniture, wall colors, and automobile features are all a part of your current value set.

If you are in your late fifties, your tastes may have changed from your early teen years. You might listen to different music, read different books, and have likely altered your decorating tastes. Your social circle has undoubtedly changed based on where and who you are during any given season of your life. Much as the gifts changed for the different ages in the earlier exercise, you shift as you flow and grow.

Want to know the funny part? You may not have changed one bit. That's the fun of an intentional life. You get to take a look under your hood and see if your engine has changed or not. If it hasn't, you can continue to build the culture in your home that supports the life you've enjoyed for years.

Here is a creative twist for pinpointing some of your values: Write a list of your pet peeves. Sounds crazy, but think about it. Write a list of five things that really get under your skin. Now look at the first item on your list and ask yourself, "Why does this one drive me crazy?" Peeves aren 't pets unless one of your values is getting rubbed the wrong way.

For example, I would probably write, "It really annoys me when people are late." Lateness offends me because I value punctuality. "I hate it when people make messes and don't clean up after themselves." This annoys me because I value responsibility and consideration. Using this pet peeve exercise helps identify some of your values.

Here are some of my current values:

SOME OF SHERI'S CURRENT VALUES

Family	Time Alone
Being Out Of Debt	Easy Dinners
Tidiness	Road Trips
Punctuality	Warm Weather
Taking Action	Friends
Peace	Faith In God
Order	Having Enough
Creativity	Clients
Earth Tones	Chocolate Chips
Time Outdoors	Mexican Food
Low Maintenance	A Great Margarita
Sleeping In	Saturday Night at Home

As you can see from my list, I value a stress-free environment. The less hassle, the happier I am. My passion is creatively making a difference. The time I need for creative endeavors and following the lives of three stepdaughters requires ample rejuvenation time. The older I become, the more I need time alone, as well as decent periods of rest. This need translates into landscaping with rocks and gravel, reducing the need for mowing. Easy dinners I can cook without a recipe means I can think about other things or chat with my family while I'm bustling through the kitchen. Warmer weather means I can jump on the elliptical or go for a quick walk to exercise or clear my head, just about any time of day or night.

The above list surprised me because it's only slightly different than my values were ten years ago as a single woman. Apparently, I have always enjoyed a low-maintenance lifestyle. Intentionally simplifying life helps support my favorite way of living, enabling me to offer my best to all the parts of life I love and value.

If you think it's important, it's a value. From landscaping rocks to being debt-free, your values shape you. Your values determine each option's worth. You weigh the options, and then make choices. Your choices become your realm of experience. You make conclusions based on your experiences, and then embrace what you believe to be true. Finally, you establish beliefs based on those truths. Every step of the way, you choose. And the choices you make determine your life's course.

STORMY WEATHER: SHIFT HAPPENS

Several components have shaped your life and continue to shape you. You choose the degree to which each of these clouds influences you. When the weather turns cloudy and rain begins to fall, you're going to get wet. Or are you?

Think of it this way: Just because it's cloudy outside doesn't mean a single raindrop has to dampen your head. You can use an umbrella, stay indoors, or wear a rain suit to keep the dampness away. Or you can don a swimsuit and dance in the downpour if you like. The level of precipitation participation is your choice. Get wet, damp, or stay dry. In the same way, you can determine how much impact you will accept from the five Clouds of Influence.

Once influence is embraced, its power will affect you, your speed, and your course. Take a look at the variation in this next diagram. Note the cloud cluster has been placed on a simple time line of your life's path.

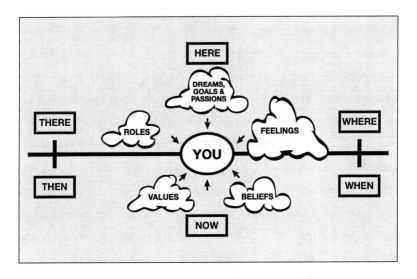

See how the cloud of Feelings expanded and even overlapped the time line? It has grown closer to Dreams/Goals/Passions, as well as Beliefs. As your Feelings increase and intensify, Dreams and Beliefs may start to feel crowded or even become blocked by overwhelming Feelings. Your forward motion slows because the Feelings cloud just fogged over your roadway. This may seem like a bit of a dramatic example, but if you've ever lived through trauma, managed a crisis, or dealt with a chronic physical challenge, you could agree it's difficult to connect with the inspiration for pursuing your dreams while your emotions are exploding.

Imagine a woman carrying the roles of Mother, Wife, and full-time Employee. Unexpectedly, she becomes Caregiver to her aging mother, who fell and broke her hip. The woman's Role cloud increases in size overnight. Now her Role cloud potentially crowds her Dream cloud. When clouds abruptly expand from a swift change, the Feelings cloud expands in such intensity it can feel as though someone took a pin, walked up to your Dream cloud, and popped it! It also seems all forward motion on your life path skids to a screeching halt.

As you develop your intentional life, this cloud/time line diagram provides two helpful assessments. The combination offers a window of understanding for why you're reacting the way you are. It may shed light on the source of frustration. The picture also provides a more realistic snapshot of how to plan for the days ahead. Understanding the weather conditions over your life map can allow you to adjust your expectations. You may have expected too much of yourself, your family, your career, roles, etc. for your current position on your timeline. With the help of a funny little cloud picture and a line, it's possible to identify adjustments you need as you continue your journey.

THE FLAG PAGE

Late in 2008, my husband and I were introduced to Mark Gungor's marriage seminar, Laugh Your Way to a Better Marriage. Part of the seminar introduces a fabulous tool you can utilize online called the Flag Page, created by Larry Bilotta. I had taken many personality profiles before but learned this tool is not about your personality; it's about your heart.

The Flag Page (located at www.flagpagetest.com) provides a snapshot of what you love most about life and helps you identify what's important to you. It is the best tool I've ever used because it provides immediate results and application to life. The Flag Page is also a wonderful source of encouragement because it shows what's right about you, instead of pointing out what needs to be fixed. The test is constructed such that you select traits from a list and assign values to your top answers; then the computer gives you a report with color graphs and descriptions.

I'll be the first to admit that sometimes I need a colored computer printout to help me understand what's important to me. Perhaps you prefer a long conversation over coffee with a friend. A spouse, clergyman, or best friend may be your best reflector during times of deep soul searching. Whichever mirror you choose, explore what you know about yourself now. Get some trustworthy feedback. What you feel and believe about yourself is powerful in shaping who you are.

NO ONE LIKE YOU

Let's consider several factors that combine to make you unique. You are a mixture of the following variables (and this list doesn't even include DNA code possibilities):

- religious beliefs

- life philosophies

- fears, insecurities, limitations, wounds, rejections, disappointments, betrayals, breakups, and losses

- screw-ups and failures

- experiences

- knowledge and training

- gifts, skills, and talents

- likes and dislikes, taste and style

- personality

- social, spiritual, and emotional maturity

- temperament

- intelligence

- belief system

- level of faith

- filters

- values

- physical health, strengths, and weaknesses

- motivators

- learning styles

- pet peeves

- frame of reference and paradigms

- geographic, economic, and cultural influences

- birth order and family upbringing/training

- time period(s) during which you live

If you were directed to mix a blend, selecting from this list of elements, the possibilities for different results is staggering. Here is the number of potential combinations represented by the forty-six factors listed:

5,502,622,159,812,088,949,850,305,428,800,254,892,961, 651,752,960,000,000,000

The chances of YOU occurring in the particular, specific mix of you at this very moment are one in . . . whatever you call that big number. Are you feeling unique yet?

WHY YOU NEED TO KNOW WHO YOU ARE

When you gain awareness of your identity, it becomes much easier to make decisions. Identity anchors you, providing a solid reference point. So when you are presented with a choice, you have a standard against which to measure. When options aren't a good fit for you, it's easier to recognize it.

Here is an example from one our family's favorite movies, *Moonstruck*. Olympia Dukakis plays Rose Castorini, the matriarch of an Italian family in New York. Rose stands outside her home with a gentleman she just met in a restaurant. The two share dinner conversation; then he walks her home. He presses her to invite him inside, and she refuses, saying, "I can't invite you in because . . . I know who I am." [3]

The line puzzled me the first time I heard it. I was living through an identity defined by rules at the time. If she had said, "I can't let you in because it's our house rule," I would have understood. But upon my first viewing, I just didn't get it.

Now, years later, I understand. She was saying, "I can't let you in because of my values. Letting you in my house doesn't stay true to who I am." It was easy to refuse the gentleman's advances. She was comfortable talking to him, and had no issue with him walking her home. But there was no way she was opening her door to him. He didn't fit with her identity or her values. Therefore he was not allowed to cross her threshold.

Another similar example is Gandalf, the wizard from *Lord of the Rings*, as he confronts Balrog, a fierce, fiery creature. The wizard strikes the rock with his staff and bellows, "YOU SHALL NOT PASS!"[4] In the same way, we each have an invisible boundary line defining our identity and values. When we know where the line is, we can defend it passionately. Are you familiar with your boundary lines?

When you are in touch with your identity, you gain boundaries. Imagine a coloring page with a picture of you. When the picture has a clear outline of your image, it's easy to know when someone colors outside the lines. If your image is fuzzy and blurred, how can anyone know if he is coloring over boundaries or not? Without a line, you don't know if you've crossed it. Awareness of identity and your position on your timeline, gives you a clear picture with crisp lines and edges. Knowing the condition of the clouds surrounding you provides clues for adaptations and changes which may prove helpful.

Several studies indicate that your personality is formed by the time you reach the age of six or seven. Dr. Christopher

Nave of the University of California, Riverside, presented a study in 2010 supporting this theory, later published in the journal *Social Psychology and Personality Science*. He said, "We remain recognizably the same person. This speaks to the importance of understanding personality because it does follow us wherever we go, across time and contexts."[5] The same journal published a study in 2003 with interesting results from Dr. Sanjay Srivastava, psychologist at Stanford University. "As you get older," he says, "you can get better . . . at least in certain traits."[6] His study revealed that women seem to improve in the areas of agreeableness (being generous and helpful) and conscientiousness (being organized and disciplined) as they age.

Your personality and behavior style may be formed by the time you are six or seven years old, but you can learn to develop adaptability in your communication, your reactions, and your responses. As a counselor friend of mine says, "The most you can ever hope to control on a really, really, really good day is you."

YOUR DEEPER YES: IDENTITY AWARENESS

Years ago I read Stephen Covey's book *First Things First Every Day*. I normally don't retain quotes, but one line from the book burned itself into my memory because it resonated so clearly in me: "It's easy to say no when there is a deeper yes burning within."[7]

The first time I read Covey's book, my faith was my deeper yes. But it wasn't until many years later I realized I am not my faith alone. My deeper yes is a much broader definition of me and includes my faith.

Your deeper yes is your identity, the truest form of you—the culmination of all your unique parts. Your faith, your essence, your flavor, your unique expression, your belief systems, your frame of reference, your culminated experiences, all combine into a complete expression of you. Your intentional life is a total extension and expression of you. It declares, "Welcome to me. You are now experiencing the core of me, the force that drives me, keeps me going, makes me stand up and say, YES!"

Anytime you find yourself thinking, *Wow! That is so me,* you are connecting with Who-you-are-now. When you know who you are, you are anchored. When anchored, you have increased awareness of the influences affecting you, so you can adapt as necessary. When you grasp awareness of the true you, the uniqueness or differences of others no longer pose a threat to your identity. You flow and bend, better equipped to adapt without compromising the true you—the current true you, that is!

Which clouds are influencing
you right now?

"It's not hard to make decisions when you know what your values are."

—Roy Disney

VALUES, UP CLOSE AND PERSONAL

You are a carrier. Whether you realize it or not, you are a carrier of values, opinions, biases, and beliefs. These principles you hold are planted throughout your day like little seeds. Each action and word sows seed from your ideological system. Just like it happens when a farmer casts seed onto plowed ground, some kernels bounce away onto rock, later to be eaten by birds. Some seed lies on top of the soil, parched by the hot sun, never producing fruit. But the fortunate seeds find rest in their moist, dark home, nourished by its richness. They take root and produce more of their kind.

Erwin McManus wrote, "Real, sustainable change occurs when actions are in response to values."[1] Every day, you produce more of yourself, based on your values. Small seedlings of you are planted through your work, your recreation, and your relationships. A conversation of encouragement on the phone plants hope in a struggling friend. Thoughtfulness is cultivated when you deliver the forgotten lunch with a funny note tucked inside, producing a young smile in the cafeteria.

The seeds you carry are produced by the values you hold. Deposits you invest today differ from what you will sow twenty years from now. Over time, outside influences stimulate slight changes, emerging as new varieties of the original seed. Corn starts out as corn, but when new genetics and environments are introduced, a hardier version of the original corn results. It's still corn, but improved corn.

This chapter will walk you through some, certainly not all, of the influences poured into you by those around you. You have been fertile ground for the persuasive plantings of others. While you appreciate some of the seeds and their fruit, others may need to be uprooted or pruned. Today is a great day for a quality check to see if you're happy with the fruit you're producing.

By the end of this chapter, you will better understand how some of your values came to be, their source, and whether or not they are challenging or cherished.

CAREGIVERS: PARENTS, TEACHERS, MENTORS

Your first encounter with life on the outside world began with people. Human hands pulled you into the world of bright light. You were cleaned up, poked, prodded, swaddled, and then held by the people who would invest in your life. Your caregivers' influence had begun.

Best friends, teachers, coaches, and mentors colored the fabric of your identity. Extended family, coworkers, teammates, and classmates significantly impacted the values you integrated as your own.

My mother was influential in my orientation to order and detail. I have an exaggerated image in my memory of Mama standing on the front porch in the summer morning sun, hands on hips, looking around the yard, saying, "Let's rearrange the farm!" (And people wonder why I have no hesitation tackling big organizing jobs.) Daddy was influential in teaching me how to handle money—saving it as well as giving generously. He and Mama also instilled a great love and respect for nature and taking care of the earth and its wild inhabitants.

The caregivers in your life gave you more than shelter, protection, and provisions. They also modeled principles you observed and adopted. My siblings and I followed different career paths, but we have the same crazy sense of humor and similar family values. We varied even though we shared the same residence, schools, parents, numerous experiences, and influences.

Your family is a tremendous force in how you are shaped during your formative years. In all its function or dysfunction, you are shaped and influenced into the person you become. You can choose your friends, but you don't necessarily get to choose your family.

SIBLINGS: BIRTH ORDER AND FAMILY PERSPECTIVE

Studies offer intriguing information regarding the birth order of siblings. Some characteristics and traits seem to be commonly found in firstborns, middle children, or youngest of siblings. Instead of pursuing these findings at this time, I would like to offer a different perspective. One would assume siblings grow up in the same family. They don't.

My friend Blair says, "Every sibling grows up in a different family." Siblings may share common events and may share a parent or two, but they can still process their experiences differently.

From the middle child's perspective, all of life was spent with an older and younger sibling. The eldest child may always wonder what life could have been like with an older brother or sister. The eldest will always be the experimental child, living through the trials and errors as he or she figures out how to be a parent.

The baby of the family may experience a more relaxed version of parental influence. "Why does she get away with that when you would have grounded me?" I know my sister and I were always surprised (and rather put out) that our younger brother got away with things we never could have done. Parents may shift in the discipline of raising their kiddos as the child-rearing years progress.

My husband is the oldest of three children. When Roger and his younger sister, Cheryl, asked their mother why their youngest brother gets away with "murder," their mother explained, "By the time you get to the third kid, you're just tired." Even parents change over time.

Siblings' perspectives contribute to the value systems they each adopt as their own. I often compare memories of an event with my brother and sister, and they remember parts of the story I completely forgot existed. We each have only a part of the story.

You will probably know your siblings longer than any other person in life. They are more likely to live as long as you do, or close to it. Investing in your siblings can produce some lifelong rewards. Sure, they know how to push your buttons because they helped install them! Though you have each grown into unique individuals, you will always share parts of life shared with no one else on earth.

FRIENDS: YOUR CHOSEN FAMILY

Childhood friendships can be fleeting or last a lifetime. There is no end to the size, shape, or style of friends who have woven themselves into the fabric of your journey to the present day. Adult friendships can be just as short or deep as our childhood relationships.

I believe friends are chosen family. You are born into one family; you design the other. You invite and include individuals into your circle. How deeply they penetrate your circle's boundary is up to you. Some friends choose to be better known by some than others.

Friends carry tremendous influence and power; they leave deposits of their character and strength in you. When a friend loves you well, he or she invests in you, like the woman who walks you through your miscarriage or the buddy from the shop who drops everything to come to your aid when you need it.

My favorite kind of friendship is the one where time and distance seem to have no bearing on our ability to pick up where we left off. It's enjoyable to have friends who don't need a lot of explanation when you reunite. Much like siblings, deep friendships can become lifetime influences.

FAITH: WHAT I BELIEVE

In the first half of my life, I participated in several different church denominations and styles of congregations. My grandparents were all Methodists, so there was a strong Methodist influence in my younger years. Sunday school and vacation Bible school are fond memories for me. For years, we traditionally attended the Christmas Eve service at my grandparents' little country church in Kansas. Some of those events are the best childhood memories I have, like the year the mouse explored the Nativity scene during the message.

We attended Congregational, Presbyterian, and Friends churches. I even remember a tiny little church in the small town of Inchelium, Washington, where we lived on an Indian reservation for one year. The church was so little, there was a sheet draped over a piece of string to divide a room in half for two Sunday school classrooms. I remember the Sunday school teacher using Barbie dolls to reenact a Bible story for my class of three or four children.

As varied as the denominations were, I learned a reverence for God. I also received a foundation of faith through the stories and principles in Scripture. Teachers and pastors modeled a living faith that captured my young heart. Throughout my personal church history, I encountered the strong influence of worship music. Sacred music impacted my musical ear—an influence that heavily contributed to my eventual music career.

Your belief or ardent nonbelief in faith and organized religion can influence all other parts of your life. We all believe in something, and your belief becomes the focus of your faith. Your religion may be football or making money. Maybe your religion is doing the right thing. Your life is a manifestation of what you believe.

I can hardly imagine living without my faith. My faith in God is so integral to my worldview that it is difficult to picture life without Him. St. Thomas Aquinas once said, "To one who has faith, no explanation is necessary. To one without faith, no explanation is possible." The nature of faith is a mystery—one I have found to be life-giving and a source of purpose and meaning.

SOCIAL: THE CULTURE IN WHICH I GREW

Growing up in the rural heartland and living in the country influenced my social skills. Growing up without a lot of neighborhood kids around meant my siblings and I spent most of our play time with each other. We primarily hung out with family and extended family. There just wasn't a lot of time spent with friends. We would make trips to town to play tennis and run around with friends in the park. Our family relationships were deep and better polished than most people's I knew.

Our family primarily resided in small, rural Kansas towns. School and church provided the majority of our social life. I sometimes felt as if I grew up in *Little House on the Prairie* or *The Waltons*. We enjoyed solid family ties, hard work, and fun that we created on our own.

On the opposite end of the social spectrum, my friend Susan grew up traveling the world because of her father's business. She grew up celebrating birthdays in other countries and learning social graces because her father was a high executive for a large company. Hosting dinners with cocktails and entertaining international guests was normal for Susan.

My cousins grew up in the military, moving to several different homes in the U.S. and overseas in their lifetime, including three years spent in Japan. They were exposed to entirely different cultures, customs, and ways of relating. Living a military life provides an interesting series of values as well.

Neither I, nor Susan, nor my cousins had any control over where we lived during our childhoods. Those choices were determined by our parents. As a result, all of us learned values based on our social experiences. Country kids, city kids, and military kids can all tell tales of how their social surroundings taught them different values.

PHYSICAL: HEALTH AND AGE

Your physical health, age, and features influence your value system. If you're twelve, you carry a fairly short life experience résumé. At age sixty-two, you have had a pretty good run through life and carry far more knowledge, experience, and perhaps some physical limitations the twelve-year-old does not own.

If you live in a wheelchair, your choices are influenced by your level of ability—whether it's realistic or not. Chronic pain impacts your values. If you are mentally challenged or care for someone who is, your choices differ from someone's who is not.

Imagine a senior in high school who is hospitalized with pneumonia. He recovers completely. He only missed some school, right? What if he was hospitalized during his state track meet? The track meet where the scouts from his dream university were going to watch him run? His vision of a track scholarship and his college future may have been altered. One episode of illness potentially colored his high school experience and his path toward college, and possibly the rest of his life.

On a much milder scale, I was recently handed the dreaded prescription for bifocals. I procrastinated getting the glasses for months. My days were frustrated by whether or not I had my reading glasses on. I couldn't read size labels in clothing.

Recipes eluded me. Squinting didn't help me read my cell phone or my iPod. One little physical influence affected every moment of my day. I finally grew weary from my little denial tantrum about getting older, admitted defeat, and purchased my glasses. I still don't enjoy wearing them. I hate having something on my face. What really makes me mad is my eyes aren't what they used to be.

Some physiological influences are just annoying and don't seem life-changing. But on a small scale, life feels different. Anytime you are forced to alter the routine parts of your day, small physical influences can feel like big changes. Large and small physical changes have the power to shift your values.

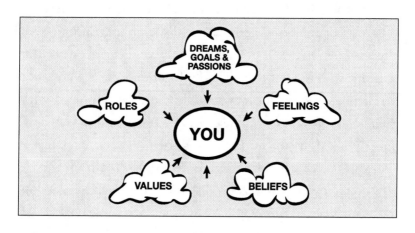

Remember the Clouds of Influence? We've spent time describing the nature of all the clouds, but we haven't discussed what's in the center—You. One important factor in your ability to flow and groove with the changing clouds around you is being a healthy version of you.

When your physical and mental health is affected by chronic pain, physical limitations, or weak immune defenses, you have an additional challenge. Healthy individuals have the strength and endurance to manage the pressures and stress of cloud shifts. Your physical skills and strength carry a great deal of impact in how you shape your values. Imagine a child who is obese, or another child who is brilliantly skilled in athletic abilities. Both children's physical condition impacts how they dress and the activities in which they participate. Their physiology also contributes to what they believe about themselves.

As a small child learns to crawl, his world changes, as does his parents'. When a toddler learns to speak, he changes the world of everyone in the household. When your aging mother loses her ability to climb up and down stairs, it changes the way she shops, attends church, and possibly gets in and out of her home. Physical influences can be subtle or severe. It's amazing to see how much we can learn to adapt when we so choose.

TECHNOLOGY: AND THE BYTE GOES ON

Technological advances are occurring at such a fast pace a computer is basically outdated when it comes off the assembly line. Our cars "think." Our phones can show us the current weather radar and anticipate the next word we type in our text messages. Our ability to handle information increases by 1,000 times every seventeen years. Computers used to fill an entire room. Now a prototype computer exists that is the size of the letter N on the back of a penny.

My centagenarion great-grandmother was born in 1889. During her lifetime, she witnessed a multitude of inventions and events of historical significance. Great Grandma Dryden was born during a time when radio did not exist. Ninety years later she owned a cordless telephone. She witnessed the introduction of the escalator, cellophane, instant coffee, and penicillin. She enjoyed watching her color TV with a remote control, but didn't want to play my brother's handheld football computer game. She just wasn't interested.

Technology continues to advance and improve, just as it presents opportunities for improvements in our quality of life. Our health care improves. We are living longer because of advances in our food, medicines, homes, and vehicles. Communication has increased in speed and efficiency. Our globe has become virtually connected to the degree that anyone can communicate in seconds with others on the opposite side of the world—in real time.

Our willingness to grow with technology will influence our values and cultures. There is a certain amount of stress involved in keeping pace with technology. And just like Great Grandma, some people find it taxing to keep up with the latest trends and advances. It seems just when you master one model, the new, improved version is released. With each advance comes new "techno language" to learn and a new button to figure out.

But when you choose to engage in the upcoming technological changes, you can find enjoyment in the learning process. Use the opportunity to tap into the knowledge of a younger generation and let them teach you more about how to use new tools. You will find some great time-saving advantages, health aids, and other advances that will be quite advantageous . . . If you remain willing to learn.

MEDIA: WHAT IS THE REST OF THE STORY?

All nations are influenced by media. Even in remote parts of Africa, Coke makes deliveries to little shops where avid fans make their beverage purchases on payday. In the U.S., we are bombarded by images and audio clips telling us what to fear, what to buy, and how our lives will improve if we do. Our cable news stations and printed publications cover the full spectrum of beliefs and political views. You can easily tune in to the station that fits your value system.

One factor in media's influence amazes me—its ability to persuade. John Pulitzer said he regarded journalism as "a noble profession and one of unequalled importance for its influence upon the minds and morals of the people."[2] I have watched several friends get hopping mad, give passionate argument, or forward e-mails to everyone they know because they trusted the message they've read or heard is true.

One of my favorite websites is snopes.com because I've found not all messages I receive in my e-mail forwards are necessarily based in truth. Before I get my feathers ruffled, I like to check the source. Before I share a story or message, I try to check its reliability first.

Be trusting. Be honest. But also be wise. I love the scripture that warns, "Be wise as serpents, innocent as doves" (Matt. 10:16).

Use the media, enjoy stories, and glean information. But in the same way writers check their spelling, we, as the readers, need to check for validity and truth.

GEOGRAPHY: YOU SAY COKE, I SAY POP

I enjoy the differences between my husband and me. Our knowledge about weather, plants, and travel differs a great deal, due largely to the areas we lived as youngsters. He knows far more than I about snow removal, even though I grew up with snow. But I know more about farming and crops, having grown up with dairy farmer grandparents. Roger and I have both introduced each other to the wonders of our cultures of origin—his diners, trains, and the Atlantic coast of New England, and my Pizza Hut, four-wheelers, and wheat fields of Kansas.

Roger gained the value of friends stopping by the house anytime living in an Italian family. My value of wide, windy open spaces is a direct result of growing up on the central plains. Had either of us grown up in different parts of the world, our values from home life may have differed. But now we have a special blend of our two worlds because we value each other, and have chosen to embrace and enjoy the other's values.

I know nothing of life in the desert regions of our country— its wildlife, its moody weather changes. But spending time in various geographic regions equips each of us with a variety of knowledge that can be shared with non-natives. Some of the cultural traditions found in the differences of our geography can be quite fun, informative, and meaningful.

CIRCUMSTANCES: NO-DRAMA MAMA

If you've raised a teen, you understand drama. If you live around a high-strung personality, chances are you've encountered drama. Drama is not my favorite way to live. Sure, I like a little excitement now and then, and a good challenge gets me motivated, but unnecessary drama for the sake of getting people riled up? Thank you, no.

Life offers enough opportunity for drama without the need to create more. This presents a problem. You are in control of you, but not the world around you. The choices of others around you affect you whether you like it or not. You have no power over circumstance, yet it seems to wield power over you. The impact of pure circumstance may be one of the more challenging influencers we all face.

Imagine you just received news and your life has just been changed forever. You may have just learned you're going to be a grandparent, or your sister is in remission. Either way, you had no control over the news. But your life course just changed.

As a child, you learned the general mood of a parent could have a tremendous effect upon the atmosphere of the home. You had no power over the environment of your mom or dad. But if there was stress at work, chances are it seeped into your home.

As a tax-paying adult, you've learned the nation's economy affects your ability to get a loan. When supply grows small and prices are driven higher, you can feel like a victim. Governmental decisions, whether you voted for them or not, make you like you're being swept down a river you never asked to swim.

Your older sister marries and moves across the country. A substitute teacher replaces your favorite classroom teacher for several months because of a family crisis. The value of a dollar drops. The jet stream dips southward, ushering in an arctic blast. A new vaccine meets the need for the latest mystery virus. All these circumstantial influences can shape you, what you believe, or the conditions in which you live.

Your values and beliefs, even your faith, are tested by circumstances. Circumstances are difficult to reconcile with because it feels you got the lemons instead of the lemonade. You want someone to blame. You may believe you are the victim. Resentment, bitterness, and cynical attitudes can find a foothold. Judgment can also become a form of defense if you are traumatically affected by circumstance. Your life is shaped and altered without your permission or invitation by circumstances proving favorable or destructive. A life shaped by circumstances alone is a risky existence.

Circumstances will affect you. To what degree they affect you is partially up to you. When you are young, you receive input naively, trusting those around you. As you grow in maturity and wisdom, you realize your own power to decide how deeply circumstances will shape you. Someone once said, "Nothing great has ever been achieved except by those who believe something inside of them is superior to circumstance."

If your washing machine breaks down, you have choices. You can decide fate is against you. You can choose to believe you are under demonic attack. Or you can decide your washing machine needs repair. It may be inconvenient and completely annoying, even overwhelming, but the washer doesn't have power over you. You have power over you. You choose how much power to give to the broken-down washer. Will it affect your mood? Your day? What you believe about life?

Filters and biases are impacted, and even installed, by some of these life experiences and circumstances. It's easy to become somewhat egocentric, thinking the way we have experienced life is going to be the same for others. We can easily float along, assuming our way is the right way, assuming everyone should experience and manage life the same way we do.

But light can dawn for you just as easily as it did for me when I came into the house one day, after doing laundry in the garage. I was living with a couple of roommates. One roommate had the habit of leaving the garage light on when she knew she was going to return soon. I, however, was taught to turn off anything that didn't need to be on. If you weren't in the room, the light should be off.

I went to the garage to change wash loads and the overhead light had been left on again. I was immediately annoyed. I flipped off the switch when I came back in the house, muttering, but as I stepped through the door, a brand-new thought entered my brain . . . her way wasn't wrong; it was just different.

I can't tell you what a big deal that was for me. After decades of thinking one way, it never dawned on me another approach might have equal merit. Her value for saving money was the same as mine. She prevented burning out the lightbulb with constant turning on and off. I'd never thought of it that way before.

We have explored several influences that have touched your life, producing values you have and may wish to keep. Their sources may have surprised you. And you've probably realized a portion of the principles you treasure came from sources you've never considered.

Now what do you do? Part of an intentional life is taking the time to look at your values and evaluate them. Much like sorting out your pantry and throwing out expired canned goods, you may have discovered some values that need tossing. Decide what is currently important. Maintain the values or replace them. Do they fit well with Who-you-are-now? Will they produce the fruit you desire to replicate? If not, now is the time to make some adjustments. If you're happy with your seeds, keep planting.

What good seeds were planted
in you?

_____

What seeds would you like to
plant in others?

_____

What is your favorite way to
invest in others?

"If you don't know where you are going, you will probably end up somewhere else."[1]

—Laurence J. Peter

WHERE-YOU-ARE-HEADED

Intentional living flows from staying in touch with your heart, your core. The constant presence of change underscores the importance of continual reacquaintance. When you know who you are and where you're headed, you can keep track of yourself and your journey.

Awareness of your identity is like discovering the headwaters of a river. Your flow makes more sense when you understand its source. When you know you're a river, you stop behaving like a pond. As your confidence deepens, it becomes easier to say no. This applies to both your identity and your direction.

We've given some extensive attention to Who-you-are-now. So far you have touched on your . . .

- themes from throughout your history;
- current roles;
- dreams, goals, and passions;
- beliefs;
- feelings; and
- current values (their level of importance, and where they began).

Now, let's connect with Where-you-are-headed by taking a quick look at your life plan, starting with your current location. Can you give an explanation for why you're on your current path? What (or who) determined your present course and speed? And more important, what is coming toward you around the next bend of the road? The path you're walking now is whispering clues about how you can be ready and how to alter your course.

HOW TO CHOOSE YOUR ROUTE

I used to be an avid power walker. I enjoyed walking for almost ten years, four to five days a week, without fail. I still enjoy it. When selecting my route, I look for the following features:
- at least two miles in distance
- some hilly terrain if possible
- as few loose dogs as possible
- a friendly neighborhood in case I run into trouble
- some sun, some shade
- options for increasing or shortcutting the route as needed

I still walk for physical and emotional health, to get some fresh air and enjoy nature. I walk intentionally. Sometimes I need to slow life down so I can breathe again. That's when I choose scenic routes, slower paces, and interesting cul-de-sacs. If I need to blow off steam and really pound the pavement, my route includes longs stretches with some inclines. When I walk, I know what I like, what I want to avoid, and what benefits me.

The same principles apply to your life walk, faith walk, business walk, and family walk. Do you have any idea why you choose the route you do? Is your path a good fit for you and your goals? Now that we've built a foundation of Who-you-are-now, let's focus on the deliberate design of your course.

WHERE YOU'VE BEEN

Just as we took a look backward in the chapter about who you are, we also will look at where you've been. When we look behind us, we learn important details that help us create plans as we look ahead. Historians remind us that understanding our past helps us wisely navigate our future.

This next diagram is one of my favorites, created by my husband. It levels the playing field for everyone. Take a look at the time line and determine where you are.

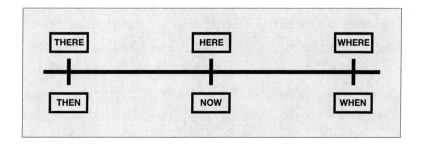

No matter what age you are, look at this time line, and you'll find you are in the center. Everyone is in the center! I remember the surprise and delight of an older friend of mine who assumed she was somewhere on the far right end of the timeline, with only an inch or so left to live. That's why I love this timeline. It's a great equalizer—we're all "here now." This timeline acknowledges your past, applauds that you're here now, and encourages your future. If you have a pulse, you have a future. You still have time to right a wrong, make a change, accomplish a goal, and reach for a dream.

This timeline offers you a glance back six months ago, three years ago, or twenty years ago. You were there, then. At this moment, you are here, now. Two questions are presented at the right end of the diagram: "Where do you want to be?" and "When do you want to get there?"

This timeline helps us remember to be realistic. I worked extremely hard and reached my goal of losing thirty pounds in six months. Now I'm trying to lose the five I put back on, plus another ten. I've been trying for three months, making little to no progress. When I look at what was required for my success last year, I can honestly say my efforts have been halfhearted for the past few months. Looking at the timeline, I also am encouraged that I have enough time to still lose something between now and my upcoming vacation, if I'm willing to work a little harder.

Look at your timeline and think of a goal you'd like to achieve. Where do you want to be? When do you want to get there? Make it realistic, based on what you know about who you are now.

You may have fallen victim to unrealistic expectations for where you'd like to be in the future. Anyone can get blindsided by a crazy circumstance that sends you bouncing along a scenic detour. Perhaps you're enjoying a steady pace without interruption, content with your progress. Based on your speed, how long do you think it will take to arrive at your goals? Does your expectation feel realistic?

Plans change. Dreams get put on hold. And sometimes, "on hold" can last a long time—even a lifetime. I planned to be married by the time I was twenty-eight. I imagined I would have a couple of children and a flourishing music career. As it turned out, my twenty years as a single career woman included more than ten years of children's music production and worship projects of my own. My musical dream came true. But where were the husband and kids?

Marrying at the age of forty-one was not my plan, though well worth the wait. My scenic route to marriage landed me squarely at the end of my childbearing years, so we immediately tried to conceive. Two years later, I resigned to our inability to have a baby of our own.

My path didn't turn out the way I envisioned. It was hard; I grieved the loss of my dream. I do love a good road trip—and this ride has been well worth its colorful detours. I didn't bear a child of my own, but I have three amazing stepdaughters and a granddaughter who is a total kick in the pants—a great scenic route. And honestly, doesn't the scenic route produce the stories worth telling?

Dreams and visions for your future cannot possibly address the multitude of variables and surprises life will bring. The future is unknown. Life is Plan B, and in some cases, C, D, E, and sometimes K. Knowing surprises will come should be part of your plan. That's the beauty of creating an intentional life. Intentionally making room for the scenic route allows you to enjoy the journey instead of dreading the drive.

Measure the distance between there/then and here/now, and then compare it to here/now and where/when. If you hold realistic expectations in one hand, and some dream power in the other, you'll gain a better balance for the journey ahead. As they teach in driver's ed . . . keep both hands on the steering wheel!

SMALL OR LOFTY DREAMS

Remember our Clouds of Influence? The Dreams/Passions/Goals cloud provides power to keep you moving along your timeline. In this season of my life, I awake each morning ready for a fight—not with my husband or my girls, but with debt. I hate debt. With our last girl in college, we are committed to paying tuition for the next several years. A long list of other debts constantly taps us on the other shoulder, and we're fighting back with a vengeance.

I dream of a debt-free life. I desire to see my girls grow up well, successfully establishing lives of their own. Roger and I both dream of living in a location near family, snow, the ocean, and a diner. We both want to be financially positioned to give generously and impact others' lives. These visions keep my motor running.

Perhaps your dreams seem beyond reach or hard to imagine. The pain of disappointment can blot out your ability to hope. Sometimes life circumstances press so hard, it seems impossible to draw a deep breath, much less dream.

Dreams can look different in the different stages of life. For the mother of a two-year-old and a new baby, the dream is a shower or a nap. For the family living paycheck to paycheck, the dream is having enough. For the middle-aged daughter visiting her aging father, the dream is he will remember.

Goals are the steps that draw you toward the achievement of your dream. Goals are easily explained, measurable, and have deadlines. Simple, achievable goals feed hope and fuel your journey. Today's victory may be as simple as surviving today's schedule or finding a dinner menu to please your picky eater. Encouragement increases with each achievement, providing hope for the next goal. Be sure to focus on realistic goal-setting toward your big dreams. One of the most powerful tools you have in achieving goals is to write them down on paper. Dreams come in all sizes, from small to lofty. Aim your energy and resources toward what you have the power to control, and those goals on paper can become reality.

SMALL STEPS MAKE A DIFFERENCE

Whether your goals are short- or long-term, each journey is a series of steps. For those of us who are impatient for results, leaping, jumping, running, and taking shortcuts carry great appeal, but speed doesn't always provide the quality journey you desire. Create small steps that fit you well.

If you want to lose twenty pounds before your class reunion one year from now, you need a plan. Position yourself for success by spreading out your goal over small increments of time in bite-sized steps. Losing twenty pounds today is unrealistic. Giving up one of your five-soft-drinks-per-day routine is entirely achievable today. Imagine how you could potentially manage a four-soft-drinks-a-day habit for a week, then three the following week, etc.

For some, the incremental slow-down plan sounds far more tolerable than giving it up cold turkey. Others prefer the cold-turkey approach. Choose the best route for you. What amount of change can you successfully manage now? Removing a bad habit in small steps really works. In the same way, adding steps of a new habit also works. Small steps move us toward big goals.

I would love to take my husband to Italy. With our financial history, it seems impossible. But I choose to believe. I want to make this trip a reality. So as we chip away at our debt, I save up for tickets, I research the best ways to travel inexpensively, and I look for Rosetta Stone's Italian, Level 1. I'm taking small steps with the big goal in mind. I do what I have the power to do now. I also trust God can open doors I can't. So I pray and ask for wisdom and His help.

Position yourself with what you know you can achieve. Push yourself to the point of challenge, not damage. Pushing yourself to the breaking point on your first day is silly. What if you snap in two on the first day? What will you have gained? Take a deep breath and pace yourself. Small steps make a difference.

HOURLY WAGE TO HONORS PROGRAM

My middle stepdaughter, Anne, took a series of small steps that stretched her—and changed her life. Anne had a track record of responding to fear with procrastination. If something was scary, avoidance was often her choice. Haven't we all avoided things we fear?

Anne took time off between high school and college. She wanted to go back to school, but it was also a little scary. She thought she'd try attending a small, local community college. But after visiting a local college fair, she came home with an armload of brochures and new excitement about college. This resulted in a weekend trip to visit an impressive university with an equally impressive tuition. After crunching numbers, she decided to look at a state college just a few hours away. When she visited the campus, she felt a great connection, so she applied and was accepted.

Anne had a record of academic achievement, so Roger suggested she explore the honors program for academic challenge. Imagine our surprise and pride when she voluntarily called the head of the honors department to ask about admission into their program. She called and made an appointment to meet with him. No hiding behind e-mails or procrastination this time! She was on a roll.

She drove to Chattanooga by herself. During her meeting, she learned she had missed the deadline for admission into the honors program for her freshman year. She expressed her keen interest, discussing options for the following sophomore year, and then came home.

The next day, Anne received an e-mail from the head of the honors department saying they had decided they were interested in her, and would she please be a part of their program immediately, as a freshman? And they offered her a scholarship. And they offered a stipend for her books. She'd get to live in honors housing, all because she took the small step of initiative to ask questions and explore possibilities. We were all thrilled.

Anne made the dean's list every semester, graduating summa cum laude, draped with ropes and two medals as she crossed the commencement platform. The day after graduation, she moved to New England and started a new job.

Who says dreams have to be lofty? Anne started with, "Maybe I could take some classes." Dreams turn to reality as you take the baby step in front of you and discover who you are. With each step, Anne was met with an open door to a bigger possibility.

When it comes to dreams, the approach is the thing. You keep checking in. Take stock. Compare your vision to your current route to determine the adjustments you need to make. Intentional Life = Vision + Decision. It changes all the time. So be intentionally aware, and start with a step, any step, toward your dream. Small steps open big doors.

STAYING CONNECTED WITH YOUR VISION

Visions and dreams and plans, oh my! Have you visited your dreams and vision lately? If you went to college, are you using your major? Have all your life plans worked out exactly as you imagined? If your answer is yes, you are in the rare minority.

I'm talking about the "What I want to be when I grow up" and the "I've always wanted to _____" dreams. Dreams seem to live with much greater intensity in the young. Their dreams are still fresh and easy to imagine.

Some of us are old enough to appreciate the bucket list—the list of things we want to do before we die. As we age, dreams fall to the wayside for any number of reasons. Dreams can temporarily be set aside because a circumstance demands it. Some dreams wither because we just don't know how to feed them. Perhaps we simply grow weary of disappointment or seemingly fruitless pursuit. Here is the reality: Many dreams will never be realized, but some will. As long as you are still on the time line, you have a future and anything is possible.

As an organizer, I often work with individuals who discover long-lost belongings in their own home because an item had been stashed in an odd place or covered up with years' worth of accumulation. When we unearth the box of candlesticks, the home owner cries, "I didn't remember I had these!" In a similar way, we need to go back and dig a little bit just to remember we have dreams—or had dreams. Life has a way of covering and burying our dreams with emotional clutter.

It's a good idea to routinely pull out the old journal, look through the photo album, visit the old files of ideas, and search for a smoldering spark of the dreams from long ago. Sometimes timing is the only thing keeping a dream from coming to life. It's difficult to pursue a dream you forgot you had.

DREAM WARM-UP

Get ready to exercise your dream muscles with this short activity. You are handed $50 in cash, with no strings attached. What do you do?

- Pay a bill?
- Buy basic supplies, like groceries or clothing?
- Pay for maintenance or repair?
- Go out to eat with a friend?
- Save the money for later?
- Get a mani/pedi?
- See a movie?

Chances are you have responded in your mind the same way as everyone I interviewed. When the amount of surprise cash is relatively small, the amount is often applied to basic needs. The result is some relief from the normal demand of living with bills and debt.

WHAT WOULD YOU DO WITH $500,000?

Let's change the number to something outrageous so you can break out of your need mode and step into dream mode. Same question, only this time, you are handed cash totaling $500,000. Seriously, stop and enjoy this for just a moment and allow your imagination to play with half a million dollars. Has your spending strategy changed? Where would you spend it?

- Pay off all debts?

- Help friends or family in need?

- Supply, repair, and replace?

- Renovate or remodel?

- Pay off loans and mortgages, school loans, vehicles?

- Pay medical bills?

- Start a fund for kids, grandkids, retirement?

- Invest or buy real estate?

- Go back to school?

- Start a scholarship or a nonprofit organization?

- Start a new business?

- Learn to play the cello?

- Make sizable donations to charities, research, or non-profits?

- Travel, vacation, play, hobbies, the arts?

- Other . . . Use your imagination?

Did the addition of more zeros help stretch your dreaming muscles? It's easy to get stuck in the rut of our current reality. Push beyond your normal mode of operation to get the dream machine into action again. Go for it.

Now look at the dreams list previously listed. Of these categories, which ones are included in the reality of your current life? None of these items is unrealistic for anyone to have in their list of goals. Even though the thought of someone handing you $500,000 right now seems outrageous, the goals of buying real estate, travel, and paying off bills are reasonable choices. As you shape Where-you-are-headed, make room for both—the outrageous and the reasonable pursuits.

INABILITY TO CONNECT WITH YOUR VISION

Imagine a casual conversation with friends over dinner. The conversation turns to the question, "What is your greatest dream?" I've seen middle-aged adults completely shift into anger, panic, fear, regret, shame, or avoidance, and then quickly change the subject when asked about their dreams. Embarrassed, or even ashamed at their inability to articulate their dreams like the others around the table, they want to avoid answering the question.

Dreams are revealing. You can learn a great deal about a person when you ask him about his dreams. While some are practiced and feel at ease with dreams, others feel threatened or exposed in talking about them. If you can't connect with your dreams, it's possible you may need some help to learn what unplugged your connection. Though I can't address every possibility in this book, I can offer one simple tool you may find helpful.

Again, start with small steps. Venture out in wardrobe, dining, or movies, and test connecting with what you truly enjoy instead of what you've always done. Try out some preferences, and learn about yourself. What kind of music do you truly enjoy? Or have you just acquiesced to listening to others' music in the house to keep the peace? Try out some things you like or think you might like. Exploration may help you reconnect with parts of your heart that have shut down due to pain or past wounding.

POSITIONING

As you begin to exercise your vision and see your dreams revive, hope begins to stir. When you lose the first twenty pounds of your one-hundred-pound journey, you begin to truly believe you'll cross your legs again. When your dog sits upon your first command, you begin to believe you will have an obedient dog.

Sometimes your journey of change begins with the simple act of taking a stand. Start acting like a person who is moving in a new direction. With little money in the bank, start saying things like "Next year, I will be rich." Those around you may think you're nuts. But when you decide you're going after something, you position yourself as though it's already your destiny. Positioning is evidence you believe! Positioning means you have a vision; you've planned the steps to arrive at your goal. It means you have committed.

When I hear anyone complaining about how she'll "never be able to ____," my next question is, "So what have you done lately to position yourself to achieve your goal?" Are you building a platform to serve as your launching pad when the timing is right? Is it possible that by saying out loud, "I'll never be able to ____" people fulfill their own declaration?

Declaration is only part of positioning. Now begin to take action by putting pieces in place that you currently have the power to move.

Let's say your dream is to paint in Paris. Are you learning the language? Are you taking art classes? Are you creating income sources to support your passion for art? Perhaps your dream is to go into medicine. Have you talked to any experts? Have you done any research on the field of medicine on the Internet? Have you volunteered time in a health-care field to test the waters and see if you have what it takes? Build your launching pad. Take-off will come. Remember the movie *Field of Dreams*? A voice speaks to the lead character while he is in his cornfield, saying, "If you build it, he will come." Take a step, a door opens. Begin building, opportunities show up.

This isn't hocus-pocus. This is faith. When you believe there is hope, you take action. God meets your faith, when you choose to believe, and He provides. Honestly, I believe He provides even when I'm a pathetic mess and don't even manage to take action.

I believe God can make a way where there is no way. I also believe I need to use my brain, my common sense, and apply my current level of faith. I've seen doors open where I never could have imagined doors existed. Remember, "A dream in motion attracts provision."

CREATING AN INTENTIONAL VOID

Another way to position yourself for taking on new change is to create an intentional void. The universe abhors a void. Black holes devour everything in their path, including light. So utilize the "power of the void" to serve as a catalyst for you. When you have an idea about something you'd like to do, create a gap, or a need; then commit to fill it.

Let's say, for example, you're interested in interior design and think you have a knack for it. So you call a friend or send out an e-mail stating you will give a free makeover consultation to the first three people who respond. You get several e-mail responses, so you determine the guidelines you will offer to each person—limits of how much time you will offer, whether materials are included, a written list of recommendations, etc. You may even offer a makeover with free labor, as long as they purchase all the materials. The hardest part of this plan is hitting the "send" button on the computer.

Why is it so hard to send out the letter or e-mail? Because you commit to the unknown, and unknown might contain failure. And failure equals pain. You put yourself on the line by offering the promise of results—results you can't guarantee. It's a risk. Are you up for the challenge of creating the void, then promising to fill it? If you're not certain, start with a smaller, more manageable step for you. But if you're ready to give it a try, just think what you'll learn in the process. Find the level of risk you're willing to meet, and do it. You'll discover what works, what doesn't, what you liked about the job, or even that you really don't wish to pursue this venture anymore. You might find out you're terrible at it—or even better than you'd dreamed.

This is why I recommend you begin with friends and family—people who already like you and support you—so you have some built-in forgiveness as you work out your business kinks. Each time I launch a new venture, I begin with people who know me, like me, trust me, and will give me honest feedback and encouragement. If you don't need the comfort buffer, go for it.

Commit to someone. Set a date. Promise a business service you will provide. Host the party, sign up for the cello lesson, or register for fall classes. Then do your best with your current resources to fulfill your promise. You will gain experience and feedback. You've begun a new adventure!

I have seen my husband jump into the void. When asked if he provides "_____" as a service, he responds, "Sure can. Will do." Then he hangs up the phone and calls the guy who has the expertise. He connects his customer to their answer. I'm still learning I'm not required to have all the answers. I only have to be willing to find answers. If I promise an answer to a client, I'm motivated to find it and deliver. If I genuinely can't find what they need, I tell them so, as promptly as possible.

In the early 1500s, Cortez sailed across the Atlantic Ocean to explore Mexico. To prevent any temptation of retreat, Cortez burned his ships—an extreme version of creating an intentional void. I'm not suggesting you burn anything . . . but when you force yourself to jump into the deep end of the pool, you are compelled to stay afloat. You might even invent a new way of floating. Position yourself for growth. Create a void. Push just hard enough that an answer or action must rise to the surface.

BLESSINGS MAGNET

We've talked about how blessings can be magnetized to you. But you can also find yourself being powerfully magnetized toward being the blessing.

Being a relatively new stepparent, I've started understanding things I put my parents through and why they did and said some of the things they did. "Aha!" moments have inspired me to call or write my folks to thank them for how they raised me, and for the values they taught me. From my new parenting platform, I have a greater appreciation for what it's like to go through all types of emotional upheaval, feel your child's angst and pain, wishing you could alleviate their stress, but grateful for the lesson learned.

My favorite delight of parenthood, one I thoroughly enjoy, is the "sneaky gift." I pay attention to my stepdaughters' current tastes and interests. When I run across something that makes me think of them—like a pack of sticky notes in their favorite color or a crazy pen with a favorite movie character perched on top—I purchase it and wait like a cat, watching its prey.

I can't wait until the next time one of the girls merely mentions the item so I can say, "TA-DA!" and present the little gift. She didn't ask for it. She didn't manipulate me into spoiling her.

I want the girls to know I care and I think about them. Surprising them with a just-because-I-love-you token tells them, "I pay attention. I listen. I know what you enjoy, and nothing gives me greater pleasure than to give it to you."

I think God works this way. He knows our interests, our likes, our tastes, the secret things we long for. I also believe He is waiting with a storehouse of great stuff He wants to open to us if we'll just mention our desire. This is one way I look at prayer. Sometimes we make requests directly out of need. But I believe God gets a kick out of doing fun things for us. I think He waits for us to just "think the thought," or waits for us to mention it and BAM! He opens the door to the exact thing we wanted or needed.

When we believe God genuinely likes us and wants to do good things for us, we become a magnet for blessings—things we like, things we're interested in—without ever directly asking God for them. Do I believe in praying and asking? Absolutely! I believe God provides through both methods.

When I was a senior in college, I imagined the wonderful classroom I'd love to teach in. I hoped to teach kindergarten, having a room filled with windows, and a big bathtub with claw feet filled with pillows for the kids to snuggle in and read. I imagined a kid-sized bathroom and envisioned some wires stretching across the room for hanging artwork overhead. I never articulated these ideas. I just enjoyed dreaming.

So imagine how hard my jaw hit the floor when I was given a tour of the kindergarten classroom following an interview for my first teaching position. There were wires stretched across the room for hanging artwork, huge windows, a little bathroom, and there on the opposite side of the room, in the far corner, was a bright orange bathtub filled with pillows. God pays attention. He listens. He knows what we enjoy, and nothing gives Him greater pleasure than to give it to us.

CHOOSE YOUR FOCUS

So let's look at where you are. As you have assessed Who-you-are-now and Where-you-are-headed, you may have discovered some changes you'd like to make. Perhaps you wish to tackle a bad habit, a sin issue, or the pain of past disappointments and emotional wounds. You may be facing financial challenges, poor health, or getting your house in order.

For the sake of example, let's say you're trying to curb spending. You've looked at your home and realized the largest contributors to the culture in your home are overspending and your retail therapy habit.

When you focus on spending-too-much, you might experience more spending-too-much because that is your focus. Repetition of get-rid-of-"X" simply reinforces "X." Practice thinking about what you do want. How do you want to spend your money? Think about "this is what I get to save, or I can't wait to give a donation to _____," instead of "can't, can't, can't" or "don't, don't, don't."

What does organizing your home offer you? Peace, more time, and a simplified abode. What does God have for you? Promises of good, blessing, and redemption. Focus on the promise of a better future. To apply this to your home, focus your vision on the new craft room or the money saved toward a vacation, to replace the old focus of "what am I going to do with this junky room?" Now your focus is aligned, and you've opened the door to blessings that will be magnetized to you.

Perhaps you've reached the saturation point and you're ready to say, "Enough! I just don't know if I can hope for a better future and believe good stuff is coming my way." If you've had a long series of bad experiences, you may be legitimately gun-shy. Right now, risk is a four-letter word to you. For that matter, change sounds like a four-letter word. You're afraid to hope it will be different this time. Even when a great thing happens to you, joy is drained away as you wait for the other shoe to drop, like some cosmic balancing machine. I've literally heard friends say, "Well, I'm getting nervous. Things have been going really well for a while, so that means something bad will happen anytime." Anticipation of doom is evidence you've experienced some pain and disappointment.

There's a difference between waiting for the other shoe to drop and having wisdom for what happens next. One makes you a victim; the other, a strategist.

SO WHAT ARE YOU GOING AFTER?

Let's take a look at the direction you're headed. Think about inevitable change headed your way. Are you entering a new season, like expecting your first baby or handing over your car keys to your newly licensed teen? Perhaps you have an aging parent or you're approaching retirement. Every season of life, every age and phase of growth, brings its own world of change.

Look at Where-you-are-headed and determine if your home and lifestyle includes preparations for the next bend in the road. How does your home support the baby's new ability to crawl? How have your time management methods created room for the family to spend more time together, now that your teenager is driving and rarely home on weeknights due to work and school activities? If your last child is headed toward college in the next couple of years, is your home suddenly going to be too big for your needs? Taking the time to think ahead will allow you the pleasure of making sound decisions before the calendar demands a deadline.

Years ago, Roger and I decided we want to be closer to New England once our nest is empty. We have prepared for several years, gradually downsizing our possessions and developing mobile careers. As a result, we feel a sense of peace and confidence because we have a plan, and our plan includes room for the variables we know nothing about. We hold our plans loosely, allowing God to make the adjustments as we journey toward the dream of living closer to the ocean.

If you have other family members in the house, will they be in agreement with the plan for the home? What if one of them doesn't want to go where you do? It's important to talk about it, allow for questions and discussion. Find out what's important to your spouse, your children, or your roommates. Sometimes compromise is necessary. For example, you might say, "I see how important volunteer work is to you. Let's find a way to build some time into our weekend so we can volunteer as a team."

Remember you are the home owner, and you ultimately determine the culture of your abode. As a leader, you can choose to honor the blend of hearts dwelling in your home. We've talked about how it's important for you to keep in touch with your own identity. It's equally important to know the heartbeat of all the members of your household.

As a leader in your home, it's also just as appropriate to say, "Here's where we're going. Come with me or not." You have to know your people—the strength of your relationship will determine the level of the conditions you can lean against it. Pushing too hard might break your relationship. Lead gently and steadily, and you might experience cooperative movement in a new direction. The reluctant participants will need reassurance and want to know "What's in this for me?" Clearly communicate your expectations and vision, and make sure you explain how you see your vision applying to their needs too.

Stay anchored in your values and beliefs. Remain plugged into the power of your vision to keep your batteries charged. Acknowledge fears that have kept you from moving forward in the past. Know your people and communicate with the people who are a part of your journey, making sure everyone is aware of the plan.

Do you see any oncoming changes ahead that require adjustment for the future?

_____

Have you given your dreams enough space on your timeline?

"A nation's culture resides in the hearts and in the soul of its people."

—Mohandas Gandhi

LEAVE IT TO BEAVER NO LONGER

If you had to describe the customs of the American family, it would have been much easier to do in the 1940s or '50s than now. The June Cleavers of the world have become a rarity in our contemporary American culture. I don't cook dinner wearing pearls. Occasionally, I wear an industrial apron, but I can guarantee I'm not in heels, I'm not wearing makeup, and I'm probably sweating with the fan set on high. Mrs. C. would be aghast.

Many of the idyllic 1950s jobs customarily implemented by the man or woman of the house are now combined or shared. The cooking-cleaning woman and the home-repair-yard-work man are no longer the consistent model. The American household is anything but typical. My husband and I are a great example. We both work. He does the laundry, cooking, cleaning, grocery shopping, but I love doing the yard work. (And I don't wear pearls while I'm doing that either.)

The current American household could easily contain a married or unmarried couple. The primary resident of a home could be a single parent of either gender, while any number of the parent figures can be working full- or part-time in the home or a corporate office. This is a perfect example of how the values of the household help determine its culture. Our American culture is unique from house to house.

CULTURE DEFINED

Your culture, whether you live in America or Antarctica, can most simply be defined as your way of life. It can include . . .

- arts
- music
- literature
- manners
- food
- lifestyle

- language
- religion
- rituals and traditions
- dress
- social relationships
- norms of behavior (including moral systems)

HOW CULTURE IS PASSED ON
TO THE NEXT GENERATION

The patterns of your activity, as well as the significance you give to the activity, become cultivated. In turn, the activity becomes part of your culture. That culture is then passed on to the next generation. It looks like this:

Pattern of Activity
Is Established

▼

Significance Is Applied
to Activity

▼

Culture Is Born

▼

Culture Is Passed On
to Next Generation

Culture can apply to a social, ethnic, or age group. I suggest it can apply to any area where humans spend lots of time—homes, cars, retail stores, restaurants, and business offices. Think about your local chamber of commerce, the local Presbyterian youth group, the local 4-H chapter, and the Girl Scout troop. They are all different cultures. They have developed ways of doing things. Their cultures become distinct and recognizable, connected to their identity.

When you invest time in any geographic area, you develop patterns and habits for the way you do things there. This can occur in your office, your home, your car, or your kitchen. The heart of customs and culture is doing things a certain way, then passing the traditions on to the next generation. Your culture grows and lives on.

Here is an example of part of the food culture in my home and how it came to be.

1984, BUFFALO, NY

Roger Bertolini is annoyed that the grated cheese he buys from the local market is "balled" due to the heat of the grater used in the deli. He purchases a manually operated Barona cheese grater. The result is the desired texture for the grated cheese that complements almost every Italian dish Roger cooks. *Pattern of Activity Is Established.*

2003, FRANKLIN, TN

Roger and Sheri marry. Roger teaches Sheri how to cook the customary Italian meals he and his daughters enjoy. Sheri learns how to use the Barona cheese grater. She also learns "the only cheese to use" is Pecorino Romano, never parmesan. *Significance Is Applied to Activity.*

2003 TO PRESENT

The Bertolini family hosts many dinners for friends and family, using said cheese and grater. Big hit. Others beg to know how they, too, may use the same cheese and grater. Alas, the grater is no longer in stores. No problem. Friends bring cheese to the Bertolini house and use the Bertolini Barona grater. Boyfriends of Bertolini daughters are trained to grate cheese when invited for dinner. *Culture Is Born.*

2009, EBAY

Roger discovers random Barona cheese graters all over the country and begins stockpiling them like a man possessed. Graters are presented as gifts to all daughters and close family and friends to pass on the custom of grated Pecorino Romano. *Culture Is Passed On to Next Generation.*

CUSTOMS: THE WAY YOU DO THINGS

As you begin to analyze the culture of your home, you will soon discover your culture is built out of tiny building blocks—your customs. Customs are specific actions, a particular way of doing things, like enjoying pizza and a movie on Friday nights, the way you hide Easter eggs for your children, or the way you park your cars in the driveway. Think about your family's normal way of doing things, and you've pinpointed customs in your culture.

We are all creatures of habit, following daily routines. When you maintain a regular pattern, you might say, "I'm accustomed to doing it that way." Note the word "accustomed." See the root word? This deep tendency to act in a particular manner is established over time, intentionally or accidentally.

The word "customs" likely produces images of international travel. When I visit your house, that is exactly what I'm doing—visiting your country. While some of your customs will differ from mine, there are some we share. One example of shared customs is the celebration of Christmas. We all exchange gifts, prepare special foods, and decorate. In fact, these same customs are shared globally, though each custom bears a unique flavor in each household and nation.

We each have a home culture filled with customs ranging from rich with meaning to just plain fun. If you compared customs in households, you'd find delightful variations. For example, birthdays are likely celebrated in most homes. But the style of celebration can vary as much as the ages of the occupants.

Your home is your own developed country—the culmination of your customs and values. As a result, your home looks, feels, and even smells different. While one home offers a casual, friendly feeling, another inspires better posture, good etiquette, and a pleasant, formal manner. Both can be enjoyed equally while different in nature.

My house is definitely on the casual side of the culture-meter. If I had to define my home's culture in three words, they would be *comfort*, *fun*, and *fellowship*. Most of the activity in our home centers on those three core elements. We use warm, earthy tones to keep things friendly and easy on the eye. Our furniture is sturdy and cozy—nothing formal. Our door is open—you can drop by anytime. If you do drop by, expect to help in the kitchen! We cook with our guests present and serve family-style. We also offer comfort spiritually and emotionally to our guests. Our goal is to provide a safe, nonjudgmental environment where you can be yourself in both crisis and celebration. We offer a listening ear, advice if you want it, and confidentiality.

Take a look at some of your favorite customs and see if they are already reflecting the values of your household. Chances are you already have several in place. Let's take a look at the customs in your home "country."

IDENTIFYING YOUR CURRENT CUSTOMS

Part of installing an intentional life is the acknowledgment of the customs already existing in your domain. If your current customs are working well for you, keep them. However, it's good to routinely assess your customs to see if they are still appropriate, representing Who-you-are-now. Some customs may have outlived their time and application.

My youngest stepdaughter, Elaine, broke with tradition years ago and opted for no birthday cake. Since then, we've had cannoli, pie, petits fours, and cobbler as her birthday dessert. Now our custom is to ask the birthday person what dessert she'd like—we don't assume it will be cake.

Maybe it's time to develop some new customs at your house. You can design and plan new customs to better reflect Who-you-are-now and Where-you-are-headed. Think of an experience when you found yourself out of your culture comfort zone. Perhaps you've attended a conference at an exclusive resort when you typically camp out on your road trips. If you've ventured across your nation's borders, maybe you had a horrifying experience, like eating a native dish still wriggling when served. Experiences like this make great stories later, though challenging at the time. Each encounter introduces a new custom to your cultural system. Someone's custom stretches you beyond your normal way of thinking or behaving.

Now imagine yourself in the familiarity of your own little abode. Think about the habits you practice in your home. Consider a time you've visited someone's home and thought, *Wow, we do that differently in our family*. Create a list of your customs. If you feel stuck, use these questions to help identify some customs in your household:

SAMPLE QUESTIONS FOR IDENTIFYING CUSTOMS IN YOUR HOUSEHOLD

1. *What are some customs you enjoy during holiday gatherings?*

2. *How do you show affection to other members of the family? Are you more private or public? What is considered appropriate for your home?*

3. *How do you typically celebrate a birthday, anniversary, or wedding?*

4. *Do you have a "signature" gift you give for weddings, birthdays, or other events?*

5. *What do you normally do when you have people over for dinner?*

6. *Do you take a consistent vacation? What time of year, and where?*

7. *Do you have house rules?*

8. *How do you normally spend mealtime in your home?*

9. *Do you routinely have chores divided among household members?*

10. *Are there topics in your home you don't discuss?*

Remember customs are typical behaviors and actions—ways of doing things. Your unique culture is completely dependent upon how you view yourself and what's important to you. When you find yourself saying, "Oh, that is so us!" you have identified a part of your culture.

GLOBE-TROTTING AND HOUSE-HOPPING

When I spent time in Athens, Greece, I stayed with a friend who was a nanny. For three days, she showed me the city and surrounding area, giving me a lasting taste of Greek culture. I almost got annoyed at how often she said, "That is so Greek." Years later, I'm grateful she showed me specific features to help me better experience and define Greek culture in a short time.

Visiting any foreign country is a thrill for me. It's exciting to leave the scope of my own backyard to experience the wonder of sights, sounds, smells, and customs of another land. I've been privileged to experience thirteen nations outside my own. At the end of each journey, I returned home with greater perspective and a new appreciation for the values and customs of those nations.

After some trips, I felt frustrated toward aspects of my own nation's culture, thinking, "Why can't we do this like such-and-such a country does it?" I've also kissed my driveway because I'm so grateful for my country and way of life.

A similar response can occur after visiting someone's home. I might adopt a custom I enjoyed during my stay, incorporating it into my culture. Sometimes the new custom works well, like removing your shoes while in the house. Sometimes the adopted custom doesn't fit with my home culture and naturally fades away. But it's fun to give it a try, and you might discover a great fit for your household.

My husband hails from Connecticut; I'm from Kansas. He came from a Catholic, Italian family who worked in sales and construction. I came from a Methodist-turned-non-denominational, Midwest family of educators and farmers. He ate linguini, seafood, and cannoli. I ate hamburgers, potato salad, and Jell-O with mini marshmallows. He drank beer. I drank pop. And that was just the beginning of our cultural potpourri.

We decided from the beginning our blended family would honor each other's customs. Roger helps me celebrate Groundhog Day with a big pancake feed for our friends, and I have opened our doors for any friend to drop by anytime. We worked hard to make sure we each allowed room for the other to continue enjoying facets of our favorite customs. We purposefully combined our cultures to create our new country.

YOUR TALKING HOUSE

Intentionally or not, you've created a culture in your home. When an outsider visits, he or she learns a great deal about you—your ways, your goals, passions, and values—even without explanation from you. Your home speaks on your behalf. Think through a tour of your house. What does your home whisper about you? Are you and your values being represented well, or did a culture establish itself without you? Sometimes lack of direction is just as evident as your taste in furniture. If your home shouts that you aren't clear about your identity or direction, then you have the opportunity to make a meaningful change.

The home that supports you will also reflect you. The alternative is allowing random circumstances to create a culture for you. If you want your home to represent you well, you must determine its message. Set the tone and atmosphere you desire.

When you walk into my house, the first thing you see is a warm, deep-red room. The wall facing you is filled with assorted black picture frames displaying photos of family and friends dear to us. You cross the threshold of my culture and it says, "We value you." Our front room was intentionally designed to speak this message to every person who visits our home. Each additional room reinforces the message with comfortable furniture and a pleasant atmosphere saying, "Please stay; we enjoy you."

As an organizer, I've tiptoed through homes bowing under the weight of crisis or indecision. The house reflects the stress and strain of its owners, speaking volumes about what their owners are bearing on their own shoulders. I've seen homes indicate trauma, wounding, and personal crisis. Other homes reflect sheer busyness or the chaos that results from the absence of a plan. Very talented, intelligent, capable people are drowning in their own four walls simply because of indecision. Organizing pioneer Barbara Hemphill draws a clear bottom line with her signature quote, "Clutter is postponed decisions."

When working with the overwhelmed, I have a marvelous twofold opportunity. First, I help the client reconnect with their heart and vision. Then, by simplifying their home, we replace chaos with peace, creating a functional home that supports and reflects its inhabitants. We create an environment that displays the values and personality of the owners. Then anyone who visits enjoys this three-dimensional representation of their hearts.

Ask yourself, "Who are we as a family?" or "What are we all about?" Consider your passions, values, and sense of purpose. When you know your yes, everything else is set in its appropriate order. As you take the time to decide whether or not your home and your way of life support and reflect your values, your fabulous process has begun. You are intentionally establishing your culture—a country to be enjoyed and visited often.

THE GIFT OF CHOOSING

The beauty of choosing a culture for your home is just that—you get to choose. We have spent time connecting with Who-you-are-now and Where-you're-headed. We've talked about culture and some of the challenges of change. Now we get to apply these elements to your home, connecting your heart to your living space.

Remember that culture is your way of doing things. It encompasses everything from attitude to value systems to the way you celebrate holidays and decorate your living area. Our next chapter will walk you through a process of creating the road map—the measuring stick—of the intentional culture you want to build in your home.

What does your house tell others about your culture?

What do you want your house to say?

"What we do flows from
who we are."

—Paul Vitale

DEFINING YOUR CULTURE

Okay, it's time to determine the culture you want in your home. The process is not difficult—just begin with the culture you've got. Let's look at what you've already established and decide which parts you want to keep, and which parts need to begin their exit strategy.

As you can imagine, there are as many cultural themes as there are people. Cultures are built upon values—what is important to you. To help you get started, we're going to look at you and your home through the eyes of a travel guide.

I, like many folks, love going to the a local bookstore and buying a book about the country I'm about to visit. Frommer's travel guides is a good example. If I'm preparing for a trip to Italy, I buy my Frommer's guide to Italy and learn all the basic Italian courtesy phrases and greetings I will need to order food, shop, or say thank you. I will read about the country's economy, their agriculture, history, special features I don't want to miss.

LOOK AT WHAT YOU SAY
AND WHY YOU SAY IT

Let's approach looking at your home and your culture like a tour guide. We'll begin by highlighting some common statements to help you identify some values that may already be part of your culture. When you hear these statements made by members of your household, you can begin learning from them as clues about the values in your home. Remember the definition of culture is when a belief or act is given significance, then is passed on to the next generation, so if you have children, pay particular attention to what they say to others, and what you say to your children. Here are some culturally revealing quotes:

- We don't do that in this family.
- You may talk like that when you're out with your friends, but in this house, we treat people with respect.
- No daughter of mine is getting anything pierced until she's eighteen.
- Save your money for a rainy day.
- Nobody gets hurt if nobody knows I'm doing it.
- Boys don't cry.
- We offer guests a place to stay in our home instead of expecting them to go to a hotel.

- We pick up stray animals and try to find them a home.
- We play when the work is complete.
- We always save first, spend later.
- Praise is public; correction is private.
- No dating until you're sixteen.
- Wait for sex until you're married.
- Always write a thank-you note by hand.
- Respect your elders.
- Recycle.

If you've ever heard yourself say any of the above examples, ask yourself, "Why? Why do I say that? What is the value I want my household to embrace or uphold?" Look behind the words and you'll find a value or belief undergirding your custom.

LOOK AT WHAT YOU DO AND WHY YOU DO IT

As you clarify your household values and beliefs, you may find you've assumed the other members of your household know your mind and agree with your "why." However, an intentional culture is spelled out carefully to make sure everyone has a clear understanding of the culture and customs we have established. Explaining your own customs opens opportunity to explaining your values.

Telling your household, "We do X this way" without the "why" behind it creates performance-based behavior. Sharing the "This is why we do X this way" offers opportunity to invest your values and beliefs. If I told my child, "We don't speak to our guests that way," I've only told her what not to do. When I explain our regard for respect, and the value we place on words of encouragement, truth, and blessing others, my son or daughter connects our actions with "This is important to my family." Always connect your customs with their value to create an understanding of the beliefs behind the act.

- Pay attention to what you say (and don't allow to be said) in your house. Articulate why you say it or don't allow it.

- Pay attention to where you spend your money. You're investing in values through your spending habits. What values are they? Talk about it with your family.

- Pay attention to behaviors, attitudes, or areas in your home that give you a sinking feeling, cause irritation, frustration, or shame. These areas are crying out with the message that something doesn't fit anymore. Something doesn't jive with your current identity, your direction, your values, or it wouldn't cause discomfort.

If you find yourself thinking, *Hmmm . . . okay, so what kind of cultural themes do I want in my home?* Here are some ideas to give you a starting point.

SIMPLICITY

I have worked in homes that have sparse, comfortable furniture, clear countertops, few decorative elements, and lots of solid colors, with a focus on texture for accents. The atmosphere of simply designed homes helps some people relax. Some find homes with sparse décor and large, open spaces unnerving.

A culture of simplicity can be determined in everything from activity level to décor. Whether you're a CEO or a homeschooling mom, building a culture of simplicity takes some time to develop but offers great reward. A simplified lifestyle applies to any age or economic status, much like putting yourself on a financial budget.

If you've ever experienced financial strain, adjustments are necessary to create relief and correct problems. Initially, the changes feel like deprivation. However, after time, you may become more comfortable with spending less. Time reveals what is truly meaningful. Budgeting is a great way to assess what is nonnegotiable and easily relinquished.

A simplified lifestyle is a way of budgeting how you spend yourself. When you take great care in committing to only one or two targeted pursuits, you gain increased focus and effectiveness. Let me paint a picture of what that looks like.

If someone placed a tin can on a fence ahead of you and told you to knock it off the fence, would you rather throw a handful of gravel or a single rock? The gravel will scatter when you launch it. Your chances of making contact increase by the sheer number of little bits of rock, but you sacrifice the power necessary for knocking the can off the fence. One well-aimed rock will take the can out and literally put a dent in it.

Your level of activity and commitments may have reduced you to a handful of gravel. Lots of stuff going on, but is there any power behind it? Just because you're active in a lot of areas doesn't mean you're having the lasting impact you desire.

By reducing extraneous activity—scattered spending of yourself—you gain focus and energy to do the job you deem most important. You can strike your target with intensity. Imagine reclaiming the time your extra activity had swallowed. When you simplify, you create room in your schedule to rejuvenate, the ability to adjust your schedule, adapting to the needs of your household. Budgeting the way you spend yourself can bring great reward, and then others benefit by having a rested, focused, energized version of you in the house.

I offer a word of caution: When you give up your current activity level to gain simplicity, you can initially feel a sense of loss. You might even feel less effective because you've become so accustomed to a high level of activity. In the same way one eliminates sweets and changes to fruit for snacking, there may be a period of withdrawal. You might miss your flurry and adrenaline rush. Over time, the benefits of simplicity can outweigh the discomfort of the initial change. You might even start a new hobby—naps!

GENEROSITY

If you are hardwired with a heart of generosity, then fold generosity into your culture. Position yourself to freely give to others. If your giving is expressed through feeding people and gathering around the table, keep your eating areas spacious, with comfortable seating. Make room for others to join in the fun of food prep if they are so inclined. Have basic key ingredients and food supplies stocked in your home to pull together a quick meal.

If your giving comes in the form of sharing goods and items with others, share your excess and wealth by donating goods to charitable donation centers. Create a regularly scheduled time each week or month when you and other family members will gather items in your home to be donated. It is a wonderful opportunity to begin to teach children the habit of paying attention to the things they use and enjoy versus the toys, books, and clothes they have outgrown or they no longer enjoy as often. Create awareness in your children about the needs of others, and encourage their personal character growth by teaching them to give.

If your area of expertise is having the perfect gift for the occasion, establish a gift closet or hutch to hold the items you love to keep on hand. Create a quick supply of gift bags and tissue, ribbons, or other gift-wrap accessories to assemble the perfect presentation. One of the dangers in keeping gifts on hand is forgetting what you have, thus oversupplying and creating an open door for over-shopping. Give yourself a boundary of only using a certain drawer, shelf, or container to keep your at-the-ready gifts. Once it's full, don't buy more. Or buy only with specific occasions and people in mind. Make sure you're able to clearly see all the items you have on hand. Remember, out of sight, out of mind is a perfect opportunity for wasted energy and money when you duplicate purchases.

BEAUTY

A friend of mine, Mary-Katherine, has a home that is a visual delight to enter. As you walk in the door, everything you see and smell is pleasant, even inspiring. Great lighting and points of interest beckon at every turn. Soft music plays throughout the home, and there are conversation clusters of soft seating in various locations, inviting cozy conversation. She and her husband also have a fantastic deck and screened-in porch, perfect for cookouts.

What strikes me most about their home is you can immediately sense a culture of art appreciation. Sculptures and paintings are tastefully and intentionally placed throughout their home. Knowing them personally, I can vouch that art and beauty are a part of their family culture. They encourage the artistic and creative bent in both of their children.

I grew up in a home that appreciated music. I recall a particular musical experience that had a lasting impact on me. My mom had a record album of *Peter and the Wolf* on one side, and *The Young Person's Guide to the Orchestra* on the flip side. I was about seven years old, and she taught me how to use the record player. I must have driven her crazy with repeated playings of *Peter and the Wolf*, because one day she turned the record over and asked me to listen to the other side.

As I listened, she narrated and guided me through the sounds and names of the orchestra as they played. Each section of the orchestra took turns playing—horns, woodwinds, strings, and percussion. As I listened, Mama suggested things like, "Doesn't that sound like a frog hopping on lily pads?" when the clarinet played its solo. After several rounds of listening to this amazing work, I noticed near the end of the piece, two melodies converged as countermelodies. One melody started with the piccolo with quick, elusive movement as the woodwinds gradually joined in the chase. Then, a stately theme of the horns marched against the first frantic theme and combined into an experience so beautiful, I started crying. I was a first-grader, and the beauty of the music moved me to tears.

My mother taught me the culture of appreciating music. To this day, I attribute that orchestral introduction as my mother's integral part in opening the door for me to be a composer. If you look back on how you were raised as a child, you may see some cultures you were taught to appreciate. Daddy taught us the culture of appreciating nature, wildlife, and art. Both of my parents were instrumental (no pun intended) in teaching me and my siblings an appreciation of beauty. To this day, their home is filled with artwork of wildlife and nature, just as mine is filled with original art and photography of friends and family.

ANIMALS

Some cultures are specialized and focused on a specific passion. I'll use my sister, Nancy, as an example. Nancy is a zookeeper. She has been an animal-lover as long as I can remember. When she was little, if she wasn't playing with animals, she was drawing them or pretending to be one. Now she directly cares for animals and actively supports the repopulation of endangered species.

Currently, she owns three dogs and a really cool cat. Her home is intentionally fashioned to serve her furry friends. The crates and dog beds are conveniently placed in the living area, and she has trained each animal to behave during the dinnertime routine. All occupants have their customs and routines for each day. One kitchen cabinet is dedicated to the animals' special needs, while a large doggie door and fenced-in yard provide lots of running space for ball chasing and tag.

Nancy's choice of vehicle, home appliances, and arrangement of her home all point toward her four-legged companions. Even her décor reflects her love of nature, as wildlife artwork is found in every room. It is easy to see Nancy intentionally developed a home culture all about her love of animals.

Notice how each example we've covered is a value—something you love about life. This is why we spend time reconnecting with your heart at the beginning of the process. When you don't know what you love, how can you create a culture around it?

Simplicity, generosity, beauty, and even animals are only the beginning of how you can choose a culture for your family. There is no end to the wonderful menu of cultures from which you can select and pass on to those who spend time in your home.

TEACHING YOUR FAMILY
ABOUT YOUR HOME CULTURE

One of the ways you can create "buy-in" with your children is by showing a genuine interest in what they love. Pay attention to what is important to them, and support it.

When your children reach the age of about six to ten, start investing in their understanding of culture by asking them about the things they are most interested in. When your son is into dinosaurs, ask how he'd like to display his dinosaurs in his room. When he's into baseball, ask him if there are some specific players or baseball items he'd like to have out as décor, or would he enjoy having a sport rack on his wall in his room, on which to hang his favorite bats or balls.

If your husband makes you crazy with the fortified wall of piled magazines and newspapers he builds around his chair in the den, ask him what he would like to use as a nearby bookcase or magazine rack for his things.

Buy into their world. Invest in what's important to them. As you validate them and what is important to them, your world becomes more ordered.

When I work with any client who shows a strong attachment to a theme or area of interest, I work hard to link into their attachment. I seek ways to honor their value of sports, dolls, Coke nostalgia, cows, or whatever their interest is. Their affection and emotional connection with their interest is an investment—for whatever reason. My job isn't to figure out why they love cows. Nor is it my job to judge whether collecting bovines is stupid or awesome. My job is to figure out how to honor the other person. I honor her by valuing her love of cows, and helping her explore options for creating a home that reflects her cow culture.

When you choose to live with others, validating them is a choice. If you choose to live together cooperatively as roommates, spouses, or as a family, you set the tone of your joint dwelling space. Intentionally set the tone based on what is important to you and the others. It requires a team effort and some flexibility, just like any healthy relationship.

DECIDE IT, DECLARE IT, AND DEFEND IT

When I first began my organizing business, I spent time working on my elevator speech—the ability to tell someone in thirty seconds or less what my business was all about. In the same way a business creates a mission statement, you can craft a statement or choose a few select words that inform others about your home culture. If you're all about cows, try thinking like an advertisement and create a slug line for your house: "The Jones Home—All Things Bovine." If I had to offer someone an advertisement for our house, it would be: "The House of Bertolini—Food, Fun, and Freedom." Either description opens the door for questions about your cow domain or "What do you mean by 'freedom'?"

One of the fabulous benefits of knowing your culture and being able to articulate it is that it creates very instant, natural boundaries for your home. When you decide as a household that you support a culture of generosity, you will rankle at the first scent of wastefulness or selfishness. When your culture embraces kindness and honesty, foul words and lies are not welcome in your home. As you take a stand for "This is what we're all about as a family" a boundary line is automatically drawn for what you will not welcome in your home.

When you get pushed by outside forces or influences, you can say, "You shall not pass!" driving your staff into the ground, like Gandalf in *Lord of the Rings*, and declaring to flesh and spirit that you have made your choice. Articulating your culture becomes a declaration of vision. You choose decisively. Then your decisiveness unleashes the power to invite or reject, to welcome or refuse. Either choice is achieved more easily when you are confident of your identity and direction.

When you draw boundaries for your home, you own the heart of your home. Do you want a culture in your home? Create it. Declare it. Defend it.

Think about your favorite sports team. They have a mascot, colors, a theme song, and uniforms, which have all become part of their distinction. They have order, structure, and character. They know who they are and intentionally display their identity. Then they defend it with great passion. If you question this theory, I dare you to wear a Redskins jersey into the Cowboys Stadium.

No matter what culture you decide to establish in your home, one thing is certain: your culture needs to be resolute. Without determination at the helm, nothing will happen. A culture will show up, but probably not one you wanted. So be deliberate. Decide to decide. Make a wrong decision; then learn from it and fix it. Just make a decision.

Show us who you truly are and what you are all about, from selecting your vehicle to how you spend your money. Choose customs that fit for the ages and stages of the people in your household. Create new ways of doing things—upgrade to match Where-you-are-headed. As your household personality grows and changes, your home can shift and adapt to be a great support system and continually reflect your unique lives. Your country is special—there is no other household on the planet like yours.

CULTURAL SATURATION: TOO MUCH OF A GOOD THING?

I have organized some homes where the children are all boys, and the entire house and garage look like a sporting goods store and locker room on steroids. I typically check in with the woman of the house immediately and ask if she needs a space—even a closet—where she can express the feminine side of her world. But sometimes the woman is just as athletically inclined as the boys and doesn't need anything to change except putting the place in order.

A hobby can easily take over an area—a room or even the entire house—if you do not guard against it. Any hobby can captivate your affection, but you, not your hobby, are still in charge of your home. You determine the saturation level of any theme. The more strongly you feel about an interest or value, the more you may wish to physically represent it in your house. Consider the balance of all the values and people in your home.

You can offer adequate representation to honor the household's interests and still have a functional, beautiful abode in which all people can feel comfortable.

I've been in homes where it felt like an explosion instead of decorating. I've seen cow themes, chicken themes, moose themes, scrapbook themes, and 1950s memorabilia themes where there was not one square foot of wall space left in any room that did not have a poster, figurine, or memento staring back at me. You can probably tell from my tone this is not my favorite method of décor. But guess what? It's your house, not mine. You get to choose. My opinion of your saturation level doesn't matter. Your opinion does. Do you like your home? Does it represent Who-you-are-now and Where-you-are-headed? Okay then.

YOUR CULTURE: A GUIDED TOUR

Before we go any further, I want to help you look at your home and family with a new perspective. Here is an exercise you can use to help describe and identify the customs and culture of your country. One afternoon, I created a Bertolini Country Tour Guide. This is a fun activity to help you discover the current culture in your own home.

Imagine your home as a country that you have to describe to a brand new visitor. Write down different pieces of information like Food and Dining, Religion, Entertainment, Key Words and Phrases, and your country's protocol. Pretend you are the tour guide and write notes that will offer help to the new visitor.

Create a thumbnail sketch of how he can best anticipate and enjoy a visit to your country. I included goofy stuff like "Areas to Avoid" like the attic and our storage shed out back.

After completing this exercise, I went back and read my Bertolini Country Tour Guide. Immediately, I noted that my first description indicated a conflict to my heart. We're listed as living in the Southeast. All of our girls live in the Northeast. The New England climate is entirely different, as is its culture. I really miss being with my own family. My geographic location needs to change, I need more frequent-flyer miles, or they all need to move closer! See how my initial reading of my Tour Guide surprised me with an element of our culture I want to change?

Read through your own guide. When you see something you'd like to change, take note. You now have a list of customs and features you can start working on to begin building your culture. (For a free Home Tour Guide form, go to www.sheribertolini.com and you can print a copy to fill out for your "country"!)

MULTICULTURAL LIVING

Many people are expertly multicultural. Before you wonder if I'm referring to my Scotch-Irish-Germanic-Anglo ancestry, this has nothing to do with bloodlines or heritage. I'm referring to the ability to shift easily between cultures.

Each household has a home culture, intentional or not. Once you leave your home culture, you jump into a retail culture, church culture, or school culture. Children speak fluent school and home cultures. Teens add youth group, part-time jobs, sports, social circles, and extracurricular to their culture collective. When you frequently spend time in a social group, club, church, or place of business, you become multilingual.

A true and worthy shopper develops a shopping culture—the way you shop, where you shop, even the time of week or day you most enjoy your retail experience. I prefer the culture of shopping at some stores more than others. Have you ever walked into a store and thought, "No way . . . " and walked back out? You were looking for a cultural fit. "I just wanted to save more money," you may say. But saving money is part of your culture, so you found the store that best matched your need.

Shopping out of your norm is not necessarily a difficult transition. Moving from high school to college or from small business to working for a large corporation can create culture shock. These larger transitions can take longer to learn. My most difficult transition between cultures was moving from Kansas to Nashville.

I lived in a rural community, population of about two thousand. My little town of Sterling, Kansas was only an hour's drive away from my parents' farm. The house I rented was old and spacious, within walking distance of the grade school where I taught kindergarten. Teaching in a public school was comfortable for me since I had grown up in public schools. The district I worked in was community-oriented and supportive. My coaching experience was extraordinary, as I had the privilege of working with a state championship girls' high school tennis team.

Moving to Nashville was like relocating to another galaxy. Now I was in a church of two thousand people, not a town population. My single occupancy of the large, old house was replaced with a brand-new house and roommate I'd never met before. Now I drove for twenty-five minutes to get to my teaching job at a private, Christian academy with different standards than my public school experience. I only knew one family in Nashville. No more farms or Midwest culture. I couldn't even see the horizon because of the hills and trees. If I wanted to go to my parents' for a holiday, it was now a thirteen- to fourteen-hour drive. I was living the true definition of culture shock.

Over time, I adapted and began to discover the riches of my new home. Now I transition easily between Kansas and Tennessee cultures, speaking fluently in both. But I have to admit even after living in the South for more than twenty years, I still feel a true sense of home when I visit Kansas—my culture of origin.

You have the power to determine the way your home functions and feels. Enjoy thinking and dreaming of the possibilities. Look at the customs you've already put in place. You may have more culture in your home than you realized. Now you have the opportunity to make changes, intentional changes, so your home truly reflects Who-you-are-now and Where-you-are-headed.

Whether you build a melting pot of several cultures or fashion one predominant theme, you can build the culture of your home—your own country. All the charm, inspiration, and deep values you hold dear can be represented in any way you desire.

Just remember. If you don't establish a culture, a culture will establish itself.

What kind of culture(s) do you want in your home?

_____

What is the next step
you need to take to make
it happen?

"When you're finished changing, you're finished."

—Benjamin Franklin

10

CHANGE

So far you've touched base with Who-you-are-now and Where-you-are-headed. You've examined your culture and are now positioned for making changes you'd like to implement in your home. Some of the changes coming toward you are totally out of your control, like aging or future real estate markets. For some, change is scary. For others, it is an open door to a fresh start. For still others, it is the great adventure.

A psychologist friend of mine, Dr. Brenda Rambo, said, "If you desire change, it means things will have to be different." But different can be frightening. Your resistance to change may be the result of your fear of letting go of the old. The old is familiar; the new is unknown. Sometimes you're more comfortable with the old. It's easy to stay where you are, even when it's uncomfortable. Sometimes your current discomfort is comforting because you know what to expect. The discomfort of the unknown is more uncomfortable than your current discomfort.

Change is challenging. Some modifications are lasting, meaningful, and alter you or your life's course. Transforming change means giving up something you've always had in exchange for something new and different, and it may or may not improve you or the situation. The changes we embrace can, and mostly likely will, rock the boat, even if the boat is just the SS *Paradigm*.

When facing any change, there are some basic principles to understand.

CHANGE IS INEVITABLE

Nothing remains the same. Change cannot be stopped. Shift happens. You can sit on the couch, remote in hand, and stocked mini-fridge at your side for the next twenty years, saying, "I hate change; I refuse to change," but even nature will get the best of you. You will age. Everything around you will have moved on—relationships, commerce, culture, technologies, belief systems, and society. The nature of life itself is fluid and ever-changing.

CHANGE IS CONSTANT

When you rise in the morning, you're slightly taller than you were when you went to bed last night. The same shoe that fit well in the morning can pinch by evening. Disks in our spines expand overnight, and our feet swell with fluid by day's end. What makes us think we remain the same?

Without change we would be stiff, static, and stale. Think about how many times change occurs. We are living beings in a constant state of change. The earth and universe continually shift and balance. Your pulse and breathing rates vary. Your eyes dart to and fro, refocusing for light and depth. Even while sleeping, you move, shift, and change position. Thoughts race through your brain each second, changing topics, recalling memories, posing questions, and analyzing details. The weather changes, and moods alter.

I love the message in this quote by George Bernard Shaw: "The only man who behaves sensibly is my tailor; he takes my measurements anew every time he sees me, while all the rest go on with their old measurements and expect to fit them." Shaw's tailor knew better than to assume Shaw would be the exact same size each visit. Change is constant. When working with change, expect things to be different. Keep checking to see *where*-you-are-now. This principle applies to navigating any journey.

CHANGE IS GOOD

Change keeps us healthy and challenged. It forces us to learn, figure things out, come up with new solutions, and hone new skills. We need change to stay alive and grow. To remain in a static condition ultimately means we decline. Muscles atrophy, skills diminish, and intellectual acuity dulls.

Think about eating the same food each day at the same time and place with the same people having the same conversation and wearing the same clothes. Welcome to institutional life— except for maybe the menu. One of the punishing elements of imprisonment is being thrown into a world of sameness. One is denied the variety and changes that the rest of the world is free to enjoy. We enjoy change or we'd watch only one movie over and over, or replay one football game for years and call it a football season.

CHANGE IS EMPOWERING

Some change is entirely out of your control. So make room for change. Plan for it. Expect it. It will come, so why not anticipate it? Prepare room for change in your physical space, financial planning, and calendar. I suggest you intentionally practice change.

Train your children to flow with change. Vary their routine occasionally to develop adaptability. If they learn early to flow with change, they will enjoy their advantage all throughout their lives. Dreading change is not a fun way to live. Once in a while, mix it up. Alter any variable. Take a different road to the store or follow the walking path toward the east instead of the westerly route. Cut peanut butter sandwiches into small squares instead of triangles. Eat breakfast for dinner. Make change an adventure, and teach your children the fun side of navigating it successfully.

Health experts say even while dieting, one benefits by occasionally eating a large meal to surprise your system and encourage it to wake up and work a little harder. During physical training, it's ideal to change up the routine of a workout to keep your body and mind from slipping into autopilot. Intentionally insert changes into your routine as soon as you realize you've slipped into a routine.

My sister utilizes this principle of variety with the animals at the zoo. She and other keepers introduce change into their animals' routines to stimulate them mentally and emotionally. Chimps are given problems to solve. Grizzly bears get a treat of peanut butter, but Nancy smears it high on the bars of the holding area so the bears have to stand on their hind legs to reach it. Bears are given giant popsicles made of fruit juice in gallon-sized ice cream containers. Chunks of fruit are frozen inside the popsicle, and the bear has to chew away the icy outer layer to reach the fruit prize inside.

Without change or resistance, our minds and spirits grow dull. Living creatures thrive with the challenge of change. Adaptability is vital to survival. When one understands how to adapt and problem-solve to accommodate new circumstances, one learns and endures.

CHANGE IS ORGANIC

Change behaves like a living, breathing entity. Think of change in light of weather's behavior. Life can be pleasant and uninterrupted for days, even weeks. But subtle changes build as temperatures, humidity, and pressures culminate in a cold front or a windy day with heavy clouds.

Change inspires growth and can also provide relief. Life needs the ebb and flow of change. Plants need rainy days as well as sunny. The earth itself shifts with tremors and volcanic activity. Weather alters and balances itself constantly.

Expecting life to thrum along without change is unrealistic. You have learned how to deal with rain and snow. You know how to find relief during long hot spells and what to do when the last frost of spring threatens your early blooms. Predictability of weather and life is comforting to some while boring to others, but change introduces variables that demand invention and problem-solving, developing new strength and courage. Rainy days and sunny days open the door to work, play, and rest. You learn to adapt and flow with your needs in the midst of your circumstances. So it goes with change. Change is not always a challenge. Sometimes it provides relief, like a nap on a rainy afternoon.

MAKING ROOM FOR CHANGE—WITHIN LIMITS

If you are going to build your culture to allow for change, it will be necessary to pay attention to your limits. Limitations are natural. The closer you get to the edge of your limits, the less space you have for embracing change. Change needs elbow room. It's like someone handing you a new outfit to try on, telling you to use the backseat of his Mini Cooper sports car to step out of your clothes and squirm into the new outfit. Limited space makes it awkward, and you can't even assess if the new pants and shirt fit well. Here are some examples of "cramped quarters" that make good changes difficult to achieve:

- *Money Limit*: If you max out your finances, you have eliminated a financial option in an emergency. If you have no savings, no emergency fund, you have limited your ability to respond to emergency needs, as well as the ability to freely give. When you spread yourself thin and overspend, you have nothing left when the unexpected arrives—the medical bill, the broken water heater, the car repair, the opportunity to spend four days on the beach with friends.

- *Living Space Limit*: If you max out the space in your home, you will have a challenge if your aging parent suddenly needs to move in, or you need to house your brother and his family whose home was just destroyed by a fire. This is when you wish you'd cleaned out the basement, the garage, and the guest room when you had the chance last fall. All the stuff in your home has crowded out possibilities of offering your space.

- *Time Limit*: If you max out your time with work, then you have just eliminated the possibility of volunteer work, or school or community involvement. Overbooking yourself means you are no longer available to others' needs or even your own without feeling you're neglecting a commitment.

- *Physical Limit*: If you don't manage your health well—I'm talking about the parts of your health you can control, like rest, diet, getting fresh air and sunshine, and exercise—you can create physical limitations for yourself. Being overweight, out of shape, and exhausted will prevent you from participating in opportunities. Playing with kids, being frisky with your spouse, and having the energy to enjoy the picnic and the walk through the park are gifts to be enjoyed. Often. Maxing yourself out physically eliminates the possibility of enjoying these precious times.

Most of these principles may seem like common knowledge but even common sense occasionally needs to be pointed out. Change will happen, no matter what. If you plan for it, and intentionally create breathing room for it, you will increase your chances of successfully dancing with its ebb and flow, instead of getting run over.

Standing on tiptoe at the edge of a cliff is not the ideal time for the wind to blow. One stiff gust can make you lose your balance. Back away from the edge of the cliff—and your limitations. Create room for options and you'll find a good fit for the changes you need.

GRACE SPACE

If you are a person of faith, I may have already plucked your but-with-God-there-are-no-limits heartstring. I believe with God all things are possible. I also believe God gives us a brain and His wisdom. I do not wish to abuse the grace offered to me by God by pushing my natural limits to the maximum in all directions, and then say, "Well, God will take care of it." Irresponsible behavior is not excused just because I whip out my grace badge and expect God to bail me out of my own stupidity. If I eat 20,000 calories a day, I will gain weight regardless of the fact that I love Jesus. Can God help me with overcoming my overeating? Absolutely. Will God allow me the joy of learning from the natural consequences? You bet.

When I receive a miraculous deliverance from my poor choices, I believe God shows me mercy. He doesn't give me the consequence I deserve. When I receive miraculous provision in the midst of my attempts to do the right thing, I believe God shows me grace. He gives me what I don't deserve.

I like to use a term I call grace space. Franklin Graham, son of Billy Graham, calls it "God room." When living a life of faith, it's always possible for God to do the unexpected, the unusual, even the miraculous. When you have a need, but you know it is far beyond your ability to meet that need, you need grace space. So you intentionally do all you have in your power to do, while asking God to fill the gap. You put yourself in the position of trusting God to move and provide for the need. (Remember how we talked about creating an intentional void? This is the same thing, only on a spiritual level.)

Go after something bigger than yourself, trusting God to meet the need. Give God room to work on your behalf. Grace space is first realizing you truly can't do anything without His help. Keep taking steps of faith and take the next step that you know to do.

Accidental living is the result of neglecting to look ahead. It's entirely possible to live in presumption. In doing so, you open the door to unnecessary complications. Building some cushion provides you with room to breathe, with a runway for response instead of a helipad for reaction. The buffer can look like extra money in your savings account, or being ready ten extra minutes before your departure time. Creating room for change can even be as simple as keeping an umbrella in each car. A little forethought creates breathing space for meeting challenges.

PREPARING FOR CHANGE

A friend of mine recommended I read Ciji Ware's marvelous book entitled *Rightsizing Your Life* because I had begun organizing with older clients who were downsizing into assisted living. I purchased the book, came home, plopped down in a chair, and dug in. Ten minutes later I was in tears.

The message struck home: Change is ahead. Are you ready? Have you even thought about it?

No, I wasn't ready. The paperback reality-check in my lap told me so. At the time, my husband and I were only a few years away from being empty nesters, and we'd never even talked about what we wanted to do, much less made any plans or preparations.

Since then, we've talked through potential geographic areas where we want to live. We've looked at real estate online. Both of us have started diversifying our income streams and have modified our jobs to be geographically independent. We have even discussed which possessions we will keep or sell when it comes time to make our next move. Now that our grandbaby is part of the picture, and all of my stepdaughters are in New England, we are earnestly pressing into the plan, positioning ourselves for relocation.

The most important step you can make is to stop long enough to gaze into the future and ask yourself "What do I want?" When you have your answer, begin preparing, positioning yourself toward your goal. Prepare for the change.

REASONS FOR CHANGE

The need for change is a constant presence. Here are some signals that indicate change that could be helpful:

- You have recently transitioned into an entirely new phase of life (newlywed, expecting first child, going back to school, starting a business, empty nesting, and retirement).
- Your children are transitioning into their next phase of growth, i.e. youngsters starting school, your sixteen-year-old getting her driver's license.
- You need to see an increase in _____.
- You need to see a decrease in _____.
- Something is creating discomfort, annoyance, hindrance, or you just don't like it anymore.
- You need a new way, a new method.
- You're stressed, bored, or feel you're in a rut.
- You're suffering physically.
- You want to simplify.
- You're experiencing a crisis.
- You're trying to avoid a negative experience.
- Your tastes have changed.
- Something no longer works.
- An authority figure has told you to make a change.
- Governing forces require a change.

Some changes, like getting older, find you kicking and screaming, dreading the aspects of the change. You can feel loss or anger, having no control over the change that's come upon you. Legitimate resistance toward change can rise quickly to the surface. We can even become puzzled by our own behavior, wondering why we're responding the way we are. It's normal to pass through several stages of resistance in the transition of change, just as you go through stages of grieving. Change means loss of something—the old way. Loss becomes grief, and grief can be expressed in anger, denial, and any number of interesting emotions. Perfectly normal resistance to change can result from any of these sources:

- fear of the unknown
- the feeling of safety and familiarity in current status
- lack of understanding or knowledge
- feeling the need for rebellion
- fear of loss
- fear of losing control (perceived or real)
- disagreement with the change

It's okay to have misgivings about change. It's normal. Talk about your difficulties with friends over coffee. It helps to be able to laugh at yourself and share the awkwardness. In doing so, your own angst is eased and you find you aren't the only one dealing with it or feeling the way you do. Find others who share a similar mind-set or find a group that seems to have answers for helping overcome the challenges.

So let's end this chapter with the great news—some of the benefits you'll find as you walk through various life transitions, intentionally or not. If you intentionally decide to pursue change—healthy change—here are some of the benefits you enjoy:

- personal growth
- learning new skills
- "*I like it!*"
- conquering fear
- reclaiming control over areas of your life
- developing new discipline and habits
- increasing inner strength and confidence
- improving health of relationships
- improving efficiency and effectiveness
- drawing closer to the realization of goals and dreams

Every day, you make choices. Every decision you make changes your life for better or worse. When you pick telling a lie or speaking the truth, it changes you. When you choose to be lazy or decide to work hard, it changes you. When you treat someone with cruelty or show him kindness, you become different inside, and the direction of your life changes. Make it a point to start focusing on the changes you've enjoyed, the changes that have borne great fruit.

As you begin making changes in your home, allow room for grace and mercy. Some deal with change more easily than others, including you. Offer yourself room to squirm a little when change is uncomfortable, knowing that the discomfort is normal. Awkwardness is part of the process as you learn new ways. Offer others in your household the same elbow room for their adaptation to new routines, new customs, and new ideas as you introduce them.

What part of your life changed today?

_____

How did you respond to the change?

"Simplicity is the ultimate sophistication."

—Leonardo da Vinci

11

ORGANIZING TO MATCH YOUR CULTURE

Now that you've done an internal inventory, it's time to look at the physical stuff filling your home. Your vision will anchor you, so let's prepare for the purge. Just in case you're apprehensive about how to begin, here are some rewards to look forward to in your organized home—your own culture.

- You save money and can earn more.
- You're more likely to get promoted.
- You save time.
- You gain space.
- You save mental and emotional energy.

- You and others benefit from your organized space and the items you shed.
- You experience less stress.
- You gain beauty.
- You eliminate 40 percent of housework in the average home.
- You accomplish more in less time.
- Your organized house sells better.
- You will find it easier and faster to get everything back in order once you establish a habit of order.
- You gain function.
- You gain a better image for yourself, colleagues, friends, and clients.
- You gain confidence.
- You recover more quickly when life gets hectic.
- You release more creativity.
- You create a healthier, safe environment in which to live.
- You regain fellowship—invite people over.
- You feel a sense of direction in your daily and weekly activity.
- Your home and all your stuff are serving YOU.

Sounds good, doesn't it?

WHEN TO BEGIN

Okay, let's review. You are intentionally creating a culture in your home that reflects Who-you-are-now and supports Where-you-are-headed. Tremendous benefits await you and your family, living in a home that supports and reflects all of you. Challenges of change lie ahead, but you're ready to engage, to set things in order, inside and out. Okay, so when do you start?

Any time is a good time to ponder and purge. When a room has been driving you crazy or you're curious to try something new, either is a good reason to begin now. You may be frustrated because part of your household just doesn't work anymore. You need an increase in time, or a decrease in confusion. Discomfort, annoyance, and hindrance are all good signs it's time for a change. Maybe you just don't like your laundry room anymore. The fact is, something isn't working for you. It's time for change.

However, the timing of your dissatisfaction can get tricky. If your hands are already filled with urgent life-demands, it's tough to turn things upside down and insert a new change into your home. Consider some timing alternatives. Look ahead for a natural turn in the road to implement change. Utilizing normal life-transitions is a great way to begin a project. It is also an excellent way to maintain your home once you are satisfied with your systems. These are perfect opportunities to check in with your vision. If you develop the habit of purging and tweaking your system each time you reach one of these bends in the road, you will find longer-lasting results. Here are some natural turning points:

The change of seasons — Purge your clothing as you swap summer clothes for winter. As you put away the holiday decorations, purge the ornaments you just never seem to use anymore, and make room for the new ones you recently purchased.

The change of sizes — Whether it's growing children or growing you, some sizes no longer apply. When sizes change, take advantage of the opportunity to purge the sizes of days gone by.

Relocation or downsizing — Give yourself the gift of two months of purging before you start packing your KEEP items.

Empty nest — You just reclaimed a bedroom. Think of all the possibilities.

Arrival of the new — Creating room for the baby, new business, or the puppy means you have a deadline to purge the old to prepare for the new. Making room for the new job may mean creating some work space at home. During pregnancy or interview seasons, take advantage of time to prepare. Toddler- and puppy-proofing forces you to critically analyze everything that lives below your knees. The presence of little ones provides a great time to sort through the lowest "layer" of your home.

Sudden loss or increase of income — Tough times can be fruitful times. Fruitful times can also be challenging as you measure what to do with an unexpected windfall or blessing. Use challenging seasons to question your use of possessions, time, and resources.

You will find you can do without a lot and learn quickly what you need to live.

The loss of a loved one — The departure of a loved one is a tremendous shift, both emotionally and physically. Rooms, or an entire home, need to be sorted and emptied. Sometimes space needs to be opened to receive an inheritance of furniture and possessions.

In each of the above scenarios, keep your vision in front of you. The emotional and mental demands of change can be draining. Without a clear picture of Who-you-are-now and Where-you-are-headed, you might feel lost in the middle of any swirling circumstance. But when you have a large anchor of vision holding you in place, you can walk confidently into a storm.

With your vision in place, you can say "Yes," "No," and, "Thank you, but not now." For example, let's say you experience an elderly family member's passing. The entire family tries to convince you to take more stuff from Grandma's house. When your vision is firmly in front of you, you can graciously respond to their offers with, "I have exactly what I need to enjoy my memories. Thank you for thinking of me."

You may not have room for the china hutch, the secretary desk, and the butter churn. Cool stuff, to be sure. But perhaps the clock from the mantel holds a deeper memory value and your mantel will provide the perfect place of honor to enjoy it. The clock fits your house, your culture, and imparts good memories. Winner.

Seasonal changes are convenient opportunities for change. If you need more tweak time than the change of season offers, here are some ideas for transforming you from procrastinator to purger.

SET AN INTENTIONAL DATE

One method I've found effective in jump-starting myself into action is setting a date on the calendar. A deadline is motivating, especially when it involves a commitment to other people.

When I decided to spend more time in teaching and training, I started telling people about the workshop series to be offered. It hadn't even been written yet. I scheduled a series of classes at my church, and then I began writing like mad. When advertisement begins, I'm highly motivated to create the product being advertised.

When you finally are able to admit you've only thought about cleaning out your closet, set a date on the calendar. Invite a friend over that day. Tell her she can watch you, help you, or just bring you a snack, but you need her there. Ask her to serve as your secretary and to itemize your donations as you fill bags, or write a list of all the wardrobe elements you need to purchase, alter, or mend. Go out for coffee to celebrate when it's finished. Build accountability, help, and a reward into your "closet date."

If you need to use the purging of your closet as the requirement before spending your birthday gift card on some new clothes, go for it. Set a date. Give yourself a goal of bagging X number of garments for donation, to be rewarded with purchasing fresh flowers. Choose a day to do it. If you know what "turns your crank," use it and schedule it on your calendar. Utilize your favorite inspirations to help you get through a small project. Use the motivating tools that work for you.

INTENTIONALLY PUSH YOUR OWN BUTTONS

When you know yourself well enough, you can work with your motivations and even your avoidance systems to help produce the desired result. This method is similar to creating an intentional void, but has more to do with utilizing your pet peeves than creating a self-imposed deadline.

I hate messes. I'm familiar with my aversion to chaos and clutter. I also know I tend to forget things. So when I need to remember to deal with paperwork, I'll put papers on the floor. I can't stand random messes on the floor, so I know I'll take action.

I like my countertops and kitchen table clear and free of interruption. When I need to remember to take my camera to work, I set it out on the counter. I don't like the "foreign object" on my kitchen counter, so I notice it as I go out the door. If I'm using my sorting bins, I set the stack in the middle of the clean kitchen table. My eye catches the "that doesn't belong there" item as I head toward the door to leave. I remember my supplies, the letter that needs mailing, or the dry cleaning as a result.

Even when I got the idea for this book, I started telling people I was writing a book. I was going to feel pretty silly if someone came back to me and said, "Hey, how's the book going?" if I'd not begun writing. Knowing how much I hate to not follow through, I started the book. Once the writing process began, I set a goal for the finish date.

CREATE AN INTENTIONAL ORGANIZING VOID

This same idea applies to organizing, sorting, and purging. Let's say your guest room has served as a storage room for the past couple of years. Create an intentional void by inviting your best friend from college for a weekend visit. Call your friend and set a date for her visit. Now you have to work on the guest room. You've offered a guest room you don't even have ready—yet. That's how you create an organizing void.

Sometimes, I will use the void method by donating an item before I have its replacement. To inspire buying the new blouse, I donate the old blouse. I am motivated to shop because now I have an empty hanger in my closet. If time passes and I find I really don't miss the garment, I save money and closet space. But if I miss the blouse, I'm much more likely to shop to find its replacement.

If none of these methods prove effective for you, explore what makes you tick. I'm offering ideas that kick me into action. You may find another method much more motivating for you. Do you like working for a reward? Find your motivator and put it into action. If achieving your vision of a pleasant guest room, a peaceful home, or a functional filing system is enough of a reward, you are poised and ready to start.

No matter what motivator you use, remember the danger of not keeping your eye on your ultimate goal. When you don't frequently check your speedometer or map, the result is often the inevitable ticket or "you should have turned left two states ago." So keep your vision in front of you. Remind yourself of Who-you-are-now and Where-you-are-headed. Everything gets measured against that.

BEFORE YOU START ORGANIZING . . .

Stephen Covey created the axiom, "Begin with the end in mind."[1] Before you launch into your project, decide what you will do with purged belongings. Trash, recycling, donations, and repairs will all be identified throughout the process. So here are the first steps of preparation you need to do—before you even begin sorting through the first zone:

1. *Have a plan for your trash*. What is the pick-up date? Do all trash items need to be in enclosed bags?

2. *Have a plan for your recycling*. Know in advance how it needs to be sorted, and have paper bags or cardboard boxes ready to haul it away.

3. *Have a plan for your donations*. Become familiar with donation centers locally, their hours of business, and what items they do and do not accept. Find out which days of the week they are open to receive drop-offs. Some centers come to you and do pickups.

(This is important to know when you donate large items you cannot lift, or if you drive a compact car.)

4. *You may also want to check with your tax accountant to find out how to take advantage of a tax deduction for your donations.* Create a file specifically for all your donation receipts and items you've donated.

5. *Have a plan for where belongings get repaired.* Research your local shoe repair, jewelry repair, appliance repair, alterations, etc. for any of the categories you will be sorting. As you sort and find items that need care, you know exactly which service to utilize and be ready to take it there promptly.

WHAT WORKS? WHAT DOESN'T?

Laura Ingalls Wilder wrote in *Little Town on the Prairie*, "The trouble with organizing a thing is that pretty soon folks get to paying more attention to the organization than to what they're organized for."[2] This speaks to the need for a firm vision as you face organizing anything. It's possible to become focused on the process of organizing instead of why you're organizing. Stay connected to your why.

As you begin, target only the areas or possessions that don't work. I'm not referring to "not working" as in "a state of disrepair." (However, if you are hanging on to broken items for months at a time, you need to ask yourself why you haven't repaired them yet.) I am referring to the parts of your life that provide a constant source of frustration, interruption, annoyance, or cause for avoidance. Ask yourself why you're frustrated. Why doesn't this work for you? You'll get to the bottom of many organizing mysteries with the simple question: Why?

FOR EXAMPLE:

1. **You never use the KitchenAid Mixer.**
   WHY? Because it's too heavy, it's stored at the back and bottom of the pantry, and you have to move five other items to get to it.

   KitchenAid Mixer storage location = not working

2. **You are late to every event you attend.**
   WHY? Because I haven't been realistic about how long it takes me to get myself and my kids ready for outings. I don't take the time to think through stopping for gas and the travel time to get to our destination.

   I underestimate time = not working

3. **You continue to buy duplicate hardware and tools.**
   WHY? Because you don't know if you have needle-nose pliers and wing nuts—you can never find them when you need them.

   Home maintenance storage = not working

If your systems are working—don't change anything. If you love storing your coupons in the second drawer of your desk because you and everyone else in the house know that's where coupons live, your system's working. Keep it! If you have all the potato chips and pretzels in a large basket stored under the kitchen island, and it fit perfectly, keep it! Rolling your towels to make them all fits in your tiny linen closet is a great way to make your space work for you. If you like the way it looks and functions, don't change it. When using your formal dining room as an office/study area for the kids works for everyone, leave it alone.

As the saying goes, "If it ain't broke, don't fix it." Focus your time, energy, and resources on the parts that don't work and need attention.

QUESTION EVERYTHING

We are creatures of habit. We grow accustomed to our ways of doing things, our foods, our schedule, our relationships, our clothes. When our routine remains unchallenged, we find no reason to change. Living in the same space becomes routine. The rocking chair becomes a fixture next to the fireplace; the family photos reside in the hall where they've always hung. After years, even decades of sameness, you don't realize how one simple change could offer more function or create a fresh feeling in your house.

Clutter can become as invisible as the ten-year-old furniture arrangement. We grow so accustomed to the presence of our stuff, and our way of doing things, we don't see it anymore. It becomes normal.

Question everything. To get rid of clutter or improve a room's arrangement, ask yourself: What area is making me the craziest? The answer to this question becomes your starting blocks for your organizing project. Compare everything in that area to your vision. Does it fit? You may spend a week or two observing, making mental note of your home and flow of life through the house. Sometimes the only answer you'll get to your what-makes-me-crazy-in-this-room question is "It takes too much time to clean," or "I just feel bored with this room and don't really enjoy spending time here." Even answers like these can point you in a direction of beginning to understand what needs to be changed.

Asking questions is an important step, so pay attention. Ask good questions, and truly listen to your own answers. It will pay off.

Here are some sample questions I've found to be effective. If you're up to it, literally ask these questions of each item in the area you're sorting. You don't have to say it out loud, but it might help. Sometimes I'll pick the item up and ask it these questions like an interrogation. It's kind of crazy, but I get answers. Address anything in your home with the following questions:

- Do you represent who I am now?
- What gives you the right to live in my house?
- Do you deserve the right to demand my limited space, time, money, and energy?

- What have you done for me lately?
- Are you feeding me or depleting me? Kissing me or kicking me?

Take a close look at what fills your drawers, rooms, closets, basement, garage, attic, and purse, and then ask these questions:

- Do I like it?
- Does it work?
- Do I use it? How often?
- Why have I kept this item?
- Do I have other items just like it?
- Can this item be easily replaced?
- Am I keeping this item out of perceived obligation to its giver?
- Am I keeping this item because I will feel guilty if I get rid of it for any reason at all?
- Am I keeping this item purely because it was a gift and it feels "wrong" to get rid of gifts?
- Is this item in style?
- Is this yet another memory item when I have 186 other memory items filling my attic? Is this one of my top 10 memory items that demands keeping?
- Does this item have value (sentimental, antique, investment)?
- Can this item benefit someone else more than me?
- Does this item bring forth painful memories or good memories?

- Can this item be repaired to working condition? Or does replacing it with a newer version seem more cost-effective?
- Does this article of clothing look great on me and make me feel good in it?
- Is this document a "lifetime" document (birth certificate, marriage certificate, certificate of divorce, deed, title, life insurance policy, etc.)?

As you can see, this list is rather long, and you may not even need the question list. These questions serve as a guide, keeping your culture in mind, to measure each item in your home.

KEEP THE VISION IN FRONT OF YOU

Life is filled with plenty of messiness without adding your own clutter and chaos. Surprises require you to find things quickly. One phone call from your bank sends you scrambling to locate the paper lurking in the bowels of your paper-strewn office. Or, you finally receive the long-awaited text announcing your sister is in labor and on her way to the hospital, but you did such a good job of stashing the baby gift, you can't find it.

When you dive into clearing clutter, several things happen. You might get overwhelmed by the volume. You can get discouraged by slow progress. You may get interrupted for a long period of time. All of these obstacles require a clear vision in front of you to stay on track. So keep your vision nearby, even if it means putting a printed version on the refrigerator.

As you sort through a room, say to yourself over and over, "I'm doing this for peace in my house, I'm doing this for peace in my house . . . there's no place like home, there's no place like home . . ." Take a deep breath. Slow and steady, determined and dedicated. You will win.

As you begin questioning everything in your home, remind yourself about what you're trying to achieve. You can quickly feel overwhelmed or hopeless if you're tackling a mountain of twenty years' worth of chaos. The goal remains the same. You are intentionally building a culture in your home that reflects who you are and where you are headed. You're connecting with what's most important to you and creating a home that tells us about what you value.

As you look at your home through the lens of your purpose and value, every category of life represents expenditures of your time. Each additional commitment or possession creates outflow of time, mental energy, money, emotion, and physical stamina. Having stuff costs. Inefficiency costs.

Shall we all live in caves and wear animal furs? Absolutely not. I like my washing machine and my flat iron. I enjoy cooking. I even enjoy cleaning up normal messes. What I don't enjoy is waste—pointless expenditure of me and my time.

The more stuff you have, the more time you spend handling it. You literally commit to spending yourself on your things to use them, care for them, store them, clean them, repair them, take them out, and put them away. Then, when their usefulness is over, you handle them several more times to prepare them for their departure to yard sale, donation, recycling, or the dump before it's all said and done.

Stuff eats time. If you don't have much time, get rid of stuff. Change your time commitments. Assess how your precious time is being wasted. Be watchful over your ways of doing things—look for actions that are redundant. Instead of tossing the shirt on the floor, put it in the hamper the first time. As you walk from the living room to the bedroom, grab the stuff on the stairway and put it in the closet on your way. You just saved yourself time for something else far more important to you.

I encourage everyone to streamline as much as possible. The more stuff you have, the more time you spend managing it. It's that simple. Stuff equals time. Granted, we have to use stuff to function and live, but stuff is here to serve us, not the other way around. None of us know how much time to we have to spend.

Finding your core, the center of what you value most about life, offers a starting point for determining how to best live life out of that core. Spend what is necessary to maintain your life—support systems around you—food, shelter, clothing, transportation, health, and spiritual needs. Then make room for the areas of life you believe are most important. Overeating, overspending, and "overstuffing" can create a wall that stands between you and freedom to live fully. Imagine wearing every article of clothing you own at once. How easily are you able to move, sit, stand, walk? Overstuffing your house has the same impact on your ability to spend your time doing worthwhile things. A healthy support system of stuff creates your launching pad for living a life you value.

Remember an intentional life is vision plus decision. Who-you-are-now and Where-you-are-headed is your vision. Everything in your life can be measured against your vision. Organizing is not the goal. It is a tool. The goal is seeing you live your life to the fullest. Organizing is simply a way to bring your vision to life.

So what isn't working for you in your home?

"Organizing is what you do before you do something, so that when you do it, it is not all mixed up."

—A. A. Milne

12

THE Rs OF 'RGANIZING

Let's walk through the process as though I were standing there with you, in your house. I will give you the basics since I can't see your specific needs. But here are some keys you'd learn by having me at your elbow, guiding you through the process.

Be sure to have the following materials on hand:
- empty boxes or laundry baskets (3 or 4)
- trash bags
- assorted sizes of zip-style plastic bags, if you're dealing with small items
- paper shredder, file boxes, or crates with hanging files, if you're dealing with office or paperwork sorting
- Basic cleaning supplies—there will be messes you'll want to clean up both during and after.

One factor that makes this process immensely more interesting is to make it FUN! Play music, and choose the time of day when you have the most energy and brainpower.

REALISM

Be realistic about how much time it will take to sort through everything. Be honest about how much time you have available. It will take longer than you think. A single closet can eat up an entire day if it's a large closet with lots of stuff. A room can take over a weekend. A garage can wipe out two to three days.

Remember that the more stuff you have, the more time it will take. Volume = Time. The bloated closet will take much longer than the sparse drawer. If you find yourself with only fifteen minutes, you might have enough time to sort out your shampoos and hair products. (Emphasis on *might*.) Unless you are practiced in the discipline of sorting and purging, my recommendation would be to begin with an hour for a small drawer and see how long it takes you to finish. Then, based on that length of time, plan your next area and see if the pattern holds true. This will give you a more realistic expectation of your pace and will increase your chances of success.

Some people work faster than others due to physical endurance and quick decision making. If you have neither, estimate double or triple the time you think it will take. As you get more comfortable with the process, you will increase in speed. Once you've completed an area, momentum builds as you progress in other areas of your home.

Be realistic about your readiness to get rid of things. You may be halfhearted about your goals. That's really okay. If you're not ready, set a date on the calendar and try again later. Talk to a trusted friend and explore why you aren't ready. Tackle only what you feel you can successfully do now. Even a little bit of progress will build momentum.

REINFORCEMENTS

Don't be ashamed to ask for help. This is the time for your village people. Call the girlfriends who will work well with you. Call upon family members who will help you without criticizing. It's probably best to involve solid relationships with healthy individuals who are objective and supportive. Select your helpers wisely.

Remember that your village people can provide physical help and stamina, plus encouragement when it gets tough. Each will offer a fresh eye, an objective perspective, innovative ideas, and options outside your frame of reference.

If invited or permitted, your helpers can also provide accountability. Solo organizing can be daunting unless you're wired for it. Play some music. Break for snacks. Make the process fun!

ROOM

Focus on one room until it's finished. Focus on the "room" in one drawer until it's finished. Focus on the "room" on one shelf until it's finished. Define the area you want to tackle, and then give yourself clear boundaries for how deeply you want to engage in each project.

If it helps, give each room or space a name. Let the name reflect the vision for the area and what it is to become. Remember the power of writing it down. Make a label with the name if that helps.

Remind yourself frequently you're making room for your intentional life. If you need to post your goals, roles, and dreams on the doorway just to help you stay focused, that's fine. Do whatever helps keep you on track.

ROUNDUP

Yeehaw! It's time to herd all your like-kinds together. I'll use bath towels as an example. Let's say you're working in the linen closet.

1. Find all the bath towels in the house, not just the nearest bathroom.

2. Stack all the folded towels on the kitchen table, a bed, or a couch so you can view them all at once. Viewing them all together at one time provides you with context. When you see all your towels and can compare them side by side, you discover what looks faded and shabby. You will discover what's missing when you realize you only have one blue washcloth left. Roundup is a great way to get an accurate snapshot of what you truly own.

3. Start with a large, general category of items—TOWELS—then move on to smaller divisions of that category—HAND TOWELS and WASHCLOTHS.

4. Now, separate all the hand towels. Stack them in color and style groupings, blue hand towels, white hand towels, etc. Separate the really ratty-looking towels that need to be demoted to rags. (Sometimes you don't even realize how your towels have become discolored until you see them against all the others for comparison.) Separate the nice, just-for-company towels from the everyday towels. Once you've grouped your separations, stand back and look them over.

5. Too many? Not enough matching sets? All hand towels and no oversized towels? Now you have an accurate picture of how many, what condition, what colors and styles. You also know exactly how much space you need for storage.

6. Do a physical count, if you like. You may be surprised at how many towels you have . . . or don't have.

Remember this roundup process applies to shoes, pencils, spatulas, CDs, note cards, sweaters, yard tools, flowerpots, etc. Use this process everywhere. Let's say you're working on your child's room. Empty the socks from the dresser drawers. Locate all socks, including those from the laundry. Once all socks are laid out to see, separate the darks, the whites, the knee socks, the ankle socks. Now subdivide the colored ankle socks from the white ankle socks.

Begin with your big category, and then break it down into smaller and smaller subcategories. See the pattern? Only then will you truly have an accurate assessment of how much volume you have of any one item. Then you know if you need to toss, donate, or even go shopping.

We pause for a brief interruption from our sponsor:

Does this stuff represent who you are now and support where you're headed?

What gives it the right to live in your house?

See how the process works? In the middle of tossing items into donation and keep boxes, you revisit your "why-am-I-keeping-this-when-it-has-nothing-to-do-with-who-I-am-anymore" standard. Check in with your ultimate goal. Frequently.

RESOLVE

Once you've herded a category together, begin making decisions in one of three directions. Have your three boxes, bags, or laundry baskets ready: Keep! Toss! Give! Sort your group of items and begin tossing them into the bins for their destiny. You can also add the category "Recycle." You may prefer to treat recycling as a subcategory of Toss. Make decisions quickly.

When you see boxes filling up with donation items and trash bags bulging—and they're all ready to go away, it can be inspiring and bring some great emotional relief. You'll wonder why you waited. But don't worry about that. You're on a roll—keep going.

Decide in advance you will deal with the easy, no-brainer decisions first. This provides quick confidence and the encouragement of speedy results. If you're really getting stumped at every turn, create a box for "Undecided," but only do this if the items are truly worthy of being given your extra decision-making attention. (Be honest with yourself—is it worth agonizing over socks?) "Undecided" is the area where you are most likely to get stuck. There will be memories and "perfectly good" belongings. You may have no idea how to make a decision.

Remember my experience in the attic? I started saying, "Do you represent who I am now?" for each object I touched. You will go through this process with your own unique vision, identity, and criterion to use as your measuring stick. Your standard will provide a steady reminder of what fits your current and future life. In addition, each person uses different methods of processing decisions, based on learning styles and sensory mechanisms. While one woman checks a plastic container for how the lid feels, another woman smells it to see if it has a funky plastic odor. The strength of your memories, processing styles, and your need to get rid of stuff will help create your basis for deciding.

UNDERSTANDING YOUR DECISION-MAKING PROCESS

While working with my friend Nell, I rounded up a group of stuffed animals so she could decide which ones to keep, toss, or give. She'd hold a teddy bear in her hands, look him in the eye, stroke his fur, look at me, and say, "He doesn't speak to me." This was her unique way of determining how meaningful an item was or wasn't. She had to touch the stuffed animal.

It's important for you to understand how you process decisions. If you are visual by nature, you may need to depend more on getting all the towels in the house together, folded in piles and set on the furniture in the living room, so you can view them all at once. Nell was tactile in her approach. I'd watch as her hands glided across the linens to determine if they'd earned the right to stay in her house. I've seen women choose blankets and quilts based on how they smell.

Don't disregard the way you reach decisions. Use the technique that works for you. If Aunt Mabel made you a hand-knitted sweater, but you can't stand the way it feels against your skin, decide where the sweater lands on your "value meter." You might gain more enjoyment keeping a tray or teapot you would use, rather than keeping the sweater that itches and tugs at your neck.

Remember that this is your stuff, so you can use whatever processing method you like. If your girlfriend, sister, or an organizer helps you sort things out, remember the most valuable decisions will be the ones you make based out of the ownership of your identity and direction for your life.

REMEMBRANCES—
THE POWER OF KEEPSAKES

One of the toughest obstacles in purging is memory-related keepsakes. The moment sentiment enters the decision-making process, progress can slow to a complete stall. Childhood keepsakes and inherited mementos become a wistful walk down memory lane, or even a painful stirring of emotion. Either way, decisions take more time.

Because we all respond differently to memories, it is helpful to have some definitive tools to deal with emotional matters. Let's look at some guidelines that offer great help in organizing with your heart.

Memories can be easily categorized into happy, sad, good, and bad. According to organizing expert and author Harriet Schechter, you can make great progress following her Golden Rule with sentimental possessions, "Keep only your most special Happy and Sad items; get rid of all Good and Bad ones."[1] I was stunned when I first read this. But her explanation totally made sense.

Schechter defines the Happy, Sad, Good, and Bad memories with the following descriptions:

HAPPY: Mementoes of positive accomplishments, joyous personal occasions, fun times, and loving relationships.[2]

SAD: Remembrances of poignant milestones, deceased loved ones, personal transitions, and wisdom gained from painful life processes. [3]

GOOD: Stuff that is potentially useful or even monetarily valuable, but otherwise not particularly meaningful. [4]

BAD: Reminders of upsetting incidents, unpleasant events, or unfinished business. [5]

HOW BAD CAN IT BE IF IT'S GOOD?

The surprising wrestling match of organizing typically appears when sorting out "Good." Why would you get rid of something that's good?

Just because it's good doesn't mean you need to keep it. Think of all the good movies out there. Does that mean you need to own all of them? Do you have room to display all the good artwork? Cook and store all the good food? Imagine the time and money it would take to invest in all the good stock or to gain expertise in every good career.

Perfectly good stuff creates clutter. You hesitate to get rid of it because it's perfectly good. Well, if it's so good, why haven't you used it? If it is merely taking up space, it's not good for you. It's costing you time, energy, and money to store it, work around it, and remember where it is. Good does not always equal good for you. As our landscaper friend says, "Any plant you don't want is a weed." If you don't want it, like it, or need it, it's a weed for you.

If it truly still has value, why not give it to someone who needs it and will use it? Donate it. "It's still perfectly good"= opportunity to bless someone else. Good stuff is great to donate or pass on.

When it comes to sentimental items, "good" is thin ice. Items labeled "good" in any form tend to stay. Their sentimental value becomes a free ticket to reside in your house as long as they like. When you hear yourself thinking, *Well, it did belong to So-and-So*, or *So-and-so did make it for my mom when she was little*, you keep it even though it isn't even our memory or anything you will ever use.

Decide what is meaningful to you. You can keep everything if you want to. When you choose to keep stuff, you commit. You commit a portion of yourself and your living space. You commit the cost and energy of keeping track of the items. You commit to boxing them, labeling them, moving them, and dealing with them. When you meet your eventual demise, you are committing others in your family to deal with all your "goods." So count the cost. Make sure your worldly goods are truly good enough to keep.

When you think about going through the attic, begin with the quick, easy decisions. Start with trash—old, empty boxes, plastic wrappers, bits of paper. Search the area for items that hold no interest to you, and cart them away immediately. This achieves several things. First, you feel a sense of accomplishment.

Second, you can already see the difference in your room and are encouraged to continue. Third, you have gained space for processing the next area.

As you peer across the room, pay attention when you see an item that stirs up strong reactions:

- heartache
- significant regret
- unpleasant memories

- guilt
- a reminder of unfinished business

Some emotions you can live without. If you are able to reasonably deal with a "guilt" keepsake or an "unfinished business" item, its departure is not urgent. Use discernment. Some unfinished business needs to be left alone. Close the door and move on. But if you believe making a phone call or writing a letter to someone will help you bring closure to an old chapter of life, you can be freed from the hook of old guilt and feel free to let the item go.

CONSIDERATIONS THAT STIR UP EMOTION

Memories stir up intense emotions that can send you reeling when you face letting go of an item that was your mother's, father's, grandmother's, etc. You can find yourself tangled in rationalizations that can keep you spinning for hours, days, or years. The swirl of emotion is unpleasant, so you want to avoid it. Avoiding a decision means you escape the pain a little while longer. When you consider getting rid of a keepsake and you hear "But so-and-so gave it to me," or "But so-and-so made it," you've likely become snared by an emotional hook. Ask yourself, "Does this item represent who I am now?" If not, then ask, "Am I keeping this item out of guilt?"

Fear is a huge contributor toward the guilty feelings we carry about our keepsakes. Granted, we may get stuck in indecision over our sentimental possessions because we genuinely don't know what to do with them. Perhaps we honestly don't have knowledge of our options. More often than not, we just don't want to deal with it because it's hard and it hurts. Dealing with our stuff requires making choices and owning responsibility.

If you get rid of your grandmother's teapot because it's cracked, badly stained inside (but it's the one you remember from all your childhood visits), you feel like you're throwing out Grandma. "How disrespectful. How ungrateful of you to get rid of her teapot." If you're hearing statements like this in your head, check for the source of the voice.

Here's the reality. Sometimes you will get rid of belongings and regret it later. That's a fact. Sometimes in the heat of battle and a surge of emotion, decisions are hastily made. It happens.

So if it feels risky to get rid of something and regret it later, why entertain the risk? Well, let's review your options. You have the option of identifying your values and deciding what kind of culture you want to have in your home. You have the option of selecting how and when you will tackle the parts of your life that don't meet your standard. The more you understand who you are and where you're going, the more likely you are to make decisions grounded in reality and vision, instead of the heat of the moment.

When you live without purpose or a plan, everything feels like an emergency. You're not able to realistically see your options—much less weigh them with a sense of balance. When you're out of balance, your margin for error increases dramatically.

Create an environment in which you are able to weigh your choices. One method is to plan to live without items for a period of time. While they are stored away, out of use, figure out if you actually miss them. Explore options for giving inherited items to other family members. Both of these approaches require time.

Here's the good news: I have never heard of anyone dying because they got rid of a sentimental item. Keep in mind we're dealing with physical stuff. These objects do not have souls or spirits. They simply represent the level of value you have assigned—or the value someone else dictated to you and you adopted. In my past twenty years, I have only ever regretted letting go of one keepsake. I've been slightly inconvenienced by letting go of two or three other basic household items, all of which were easily replaced.

I truly believe people and experiences become a part of us—the fabric of who we are. The belongings passed on to us by those we love are just stuff. The person is valuable. The memory of the person and your time with them is precious. The keepsake is simply a key that opens the door to your memory. Identify your best memories and give them a place of honor in your home. Enjoy your memories, knowing that person or experience is a part of you. The token may crumble and decay, but who you are now is the result of those who've loved you and invested in you—that cannot be taken away.

THE WHEAT BUCKET

When I moved to Nashville in 1988, I brought a piece of Kansas with me. Both of my grandfathers farmed wheat, and each had given me a bundle from their harvest that summer. I combined the two bunches and placed them in a tall, wooden bucket. It looked really cool.

Now jump forward more than twenty years later, and I still had the bucket of wheat. Spiders, cobwebs, and all.

I managed to avoid making a decision about the wheat. The bucket swallowed a lot of floor space in our front room, and I didn't give it the cleaning attention it deserved. Finally it dawned on me I didn't need the entire bucket to remember Kansas and my grandfathers. A few select stalks of wheat could display nicely in a shadow box that would be spider-free. This sounded like a brilliant plan, so I gathered a trash can and the wheat and began selecting the stalks to keep.

As I shoved the first few broken stalks into the trash, tears started to flow. The next minute, I was bawling. My stepdaughter, Anne, asked if she could help me in any way. I was as surprised as she how this process was affecting me. I asked her to stay with me as I sorted out enough wheat to give to my brother and sister, and kept some for myself. The remaining stalks were forced into the trash while I cried.

Why hadn't I done this before now? I wasn't being lazy. I was avoiding pain. The potential for facing a flood of memories was just under the surface—the loss of both grandfathers and my homesickness for Kansas. Avoiding the wheat protected me from remembering, shielding me from the pain of loss and separation. The act of purging the wheat felt like I was dumping my history, discarding the memories of my grandfathers. I confessed to Anne I felt like I was betraying them.

Purging a possession from my past forced me to revisit a sense of loss. An inanimate object had the power to pull forward ancient emotions—raw emotions tumbling into the present moment with the same intensity they'd held years ago.

I marvel at how our minds and emotions attach such powerful feelings to objects. As I jammed the last of the wheat into the trash, I had a strange, fleeting thought. The act of putting a once-valued keepsake into the garbage translated into dishonoring my Kansan history. That's what it felt like but it wasn't the truth.

The truth is, I still hold every memory of my grandparents. I remember riding on the combine with Grandpa or my Uncle Don, then romping through the wheat kernels, tanned and barefooted, along with my cousins in the back of the wheat truck. I am—and always will be—a Kansas girl regardless of my address. Those memories will be with me forever. They remain whether I have a bucket of wheat or not.

The other reality check was I needed to reduce the size of the spider real estate sitting in our front room. So I chose to face a potentially painful process only lasting a few minutes. Now my siblings and I will spend years enjoying the gift of wheat in a shadow box reflecting our summers on a Kansas farm. The pleasures of my memories are intact. Plus, I gained a little more floor space in my house—and fewer spiders!

RUNNING INTO GUILT

Some decisions prove difficult due to feelings of guilt. "Guilt possessions" are often sentimentally based, but not always. Gifts often fall into the guilt-category. The ugly clock, the sweater you never liked, the antique your best friend just knew you had to have. You can't decide what to do with the gift or the keepsake because you feel guilty about passing it on or tossing it. Here's some interesting insight I've recently learned about guilt.

I receive an e-mail newsletter from Linda Spangle, author of the book *Life Is Hard, Food Is Easy*. In one of her e-mails, I found a new perspective on feeling guilty. Linda suggests, when you say, "I feel guilty," you are not describing a feeling. Instead, the word is a general cover for other emotions. She recommends you ask the question, "If I wasn't feeling guilty, what would I be feeling?"[6] You may find you're feeling any combination of the following emotions:

- Disappointment
- Embarrassment
- Frustration
- Fear
- Anger
- Worry
- Resentment

When you lift the lid off guilt, you find its emotional sources beneath. When you can name them, you can deal with them. When you understand, you can take action. Guilt is a handy decoy for avoiding real heart issues. Knowing the real contributors of your angst, and knowing them by their names, is the beginning of unplugging their power over you.

Think of an item you've kept due to feelings of guilt. Dig below the guilt. What are you really feeling? If you were given permission to say what you really feel about this item, what would you say? Owning your own feelings is a vital part of managing your memories. When you truly identify how you feel about an item, you can make a much more balanced decision regarding its departure or continued presence in your home.

Okay, now we've given you some equipment for working with guilt, let's move back into our list of Rs.

REASSESS

Once you have established what to keep, assess how much room you need for storage and what kind of containment you need. Make sure you have enough room in your dresser drawer and plenty of hanging space in your closet for the garments you've kept. Utilize the space under your bed for off-season items or shoes. Is your pantry large enough to store the small appliances and foods? Test the spaces you have for storing the clothing you've kept, and then adjust as necessary in the next R step. Maybe you need to get rid of more, maybe not!

RESTRICTION

As often as possible, try to put one category of item in any one container or pile while sorting. It's okay to have a miscellaneous box when you just can't decide what category an item fits in, but try to keep tossing into this box at a minimum.

Give yourself limits. Limit the time you can take for making decisions; limit the amount of items you can keep and the size of container you can use to store "x." Set reasonable boundaries for yourself, housing an appropriate volume for your culture. (In more stressful circumstances, like sorting through the estate after the loss of a family member, you may need to adjust how you handle restrictions.)

You may decide, even though you have thirty pairs of shoes in your Keep pile, you only want to use the existing shelves in your closet and not crowd your hanging space by installing more shoe shelves. So go back to your Keep shoes and whittle down the selection (sigh) to the number of shoes that will comfortably fit on your existing shelves. Or you can reassess other areas in your home where the rest of your shoes could live. Most space is negotiable. Live comfortably within your current limits of space, or change your space to fit your belongings. Either way works.

RUBBERMAID

I am not endorsing the manufacturer as much as I'm referring to containers. (I just wanted to use another word that began with *R*.) The main idea is containment, containment, containment.

One of my male customers confessed that he always wondered who in the world bought all that container stuff he'd see in stores. He just didn't get it. After I had coached him and his wife for a couple of weeks, he said that now he is a total container fan. He revolutionized the storage in his attic, using clear containers. There are tons of great advantages you gain when you "containerize."

Containers give you an immediate visual cue about what lives inside. It communicates to you and everyone else in the house, "This is where _____ lives." When you can see where a category lives, you are more likely to put it there.

Containers create natural boundaries. Four sides and a lid create an automatic limitation to the volume of what you can store inside. Subconsciously, your brain sees a boundary. (And yes, if all your stuff doesn't fit, some see an opportunity to buy another container to hold even more stuff!) When you store your bath products in a nice bin and it works well for you, you may find that the comfort of your container system helps discourage your tendency to overbuy, overstuff, or over-keep. Once the container is full, use what you have. Don't buy more.

For children, containers offer a wonderful boundary that helps teach appropriate amounts. Offer your child a container with a lid and tell her she can keep as many stuffed animals as will fit in the container, but the lid has to snap closed easily. Watch how she processes her decisions. The child applies her own value system for which toys hold more importance. When the container is almost full and ten stuffed animals are still waiting their turn, suddenly some animals become more important than others. One animal gets pulled out of the bin while another gets chosen to stay. You didn't have to be the "bad guy" . . . the container was the guide—a natural limitation.

Containers help protect their contents from critters and dust. You also avoid the natural decay of cardboard—an invitation for critters, dust, not to mention an open invitation to mold in damp conditions.

Instant mobility is one of my favorite advantages of using containers for storage. When you need to move the hair products from one bathroom to another, just pick up the container and move it. You don't have to pick up twelve individual bottles of hair product. When loose items are housed in a bin or basket, cleaning is a breeze: Pick up the container. Wipe off the shelf. Put container back on the shelf. Would you prefer to pick up each item off the shelf, find another place to set them all down, clean the shelf, and then replace each item back on the shelf? I have better things to do with my time, as I'm sure you do!

Using plastic bins in bathrooms is a total plus simply because they prevent messes from spreading. One container storing shampoo or lotion bottles holds back the goo. Leaking hair conditioner can't drip onto all the shelves or seep into other containers. Cleaning one bin is far easier than cleaning all the shelves and contents below the leak!

For the most part, containers are relatively inexpensive and will probably last as long as the items they store—that is, until your tastes change or your daughter takes them all to college with her. Just remember that it's a good idea to do all your purging and sorting before you buy containers. Only then will you know how much product will need to be stored and you'll be able to look for appropriates sizes that fit the contents and the spaces where you'll be storing your goods.

RELOCATION

Once you have decided an item serves you, makes you look good, provides a worthy memory, or can never be replaced, you have good reasons for keeping it. The next question is, where? Establish the best location for the belongings you have sorted. Just because they came out of the hall closet doesn't mean they automatically go back into the same closet. Question everything. Does it make more sense for the umbrellas to live in the back porch or the hall closet? Look at your flow of life for each group of items and determine if this truly is where they need to live.

Every book, paper clip, CD, photograph, document, chair, lamp, table, spoon, cookie sheet, and dog leash lives somewhere.

- Does this item live in a place that makes sense for its use and frequency of use?

- Does this item live in a place where I can access it easily?

- Does this item live in a place that makes sense? (Does the dog leash live near the door where you go out to take the dog for a walk? Is the stain remover in the laundry room, where you remove stains? Are the buttons in a sewing basket, and CDs near the CD player?)

- Does this item live in a place where its needs are met (temperature, humidity, protection from dust, darkness, or light, etc.)?

- Does this item play well with others like it? Do cords keep getting tangled up together? Are paper clips and push pins together and poking your finger whenever you reach for a paper clip? Perhaps a different method of storage will prevent the tangles and pokes.

- Is this a heavy item (keep it low) or a lightweight item (store it high)?

As you determine the home of your possessions, give the area a name. Remember names are powerful as a learning tool and a point of destiny. People and things live up to their names. I believe there is a spiritual principle behind the power within a name—a magnetic pull—that provides a sense of destiny.

A lot of time and thought are invested in deciding the name of a new baby, a business, or a book title. Names bear a tremendous amount of meaning. So utilize the natural power of names by assigning names to rooms, spaces, even shelves. I have the "crunchy, salty" shelf in my pantry. The "queen-sized" shelf in my linen closet holdzs all the queen linens, while the "twin-sized" shelf holds the smaller sheet sets. We have a Family Room, the

Medicine basket, and the Paper Goods bin. Each has a name, so members of the house know its function. Items are much likelier to find their way back to their home because everyone understands the purpose of the space due to its name.

REMOVE

Chances are you now have piles of stuff that need to go away. Don't allow them to sit in your garage for weeks, or sit in your car for the next several days, or sit on the kitchen table. You've taken action to get this far. Keep going! Complete the task of putting the discarded items where they belong next.

You have many options for where your discarded items can live next. I am a firm believer in recycling—not just paper, plastic, and glass—but also recycling items in good-to-excellent condition, allowing others to own the item and get more good use out of it. There are a number of ways to find new homes for our unwanted items:

The dump—if it's trash, call it trash. Don't take it to a donation center.

Hazardous waste—Take chemicals, batteries, paints, computers and electronics, and fluorescent bulbs to a local facility designed for containment. If no local services are available, check with your city or county offices to learn about services available for disposal of hazardous materials.

Recycling Centers—Take glass, plastics, cardboard, mixed paper, tin, and aluminum to your local recycling location. Garden containers can often be returned to local garden centers or nurseries where the plants were purchased. Wire hangers from dry-cleaning services are often welcomed when returned to your local dry cleaner.

Family or friends—have a giveaway night. Invite folks to your house and let them choose from the items you're giving away. Have a clothing swap, a garage swap, or a kitchen swap. Some items rarely used in one home may be the current need in another home. If you've been hanging on to specific articles to give to designated family members at a later time, box them and send them now, so they're not underfoot and eating up your daily life space.

Goodwill, Salvation Army, and other charitable donation centers—please honor the donation centers and those who shop and work there by giving them decent items. Call in advance to find out what items they accept and their days and hours of operation. Some centers have many drop-off locations, while others will even send a truck to your home to pick up your donations.

Yard sale—this can be fun. It is also work intensive and may not be cost-effective unless you have a great area, a good showing, and lots of high-ticket items. If you have the manpower and the energy, go for it.

Craigslist.org—this option offers a free listing for forty-five days. I recommend you try this first, and then try consignment if it doesn't sell. Using Craigslist works best if you have the time and computer know-how for loading a good photo and description of your item. You have to be available to potential buyers. But it's cool—you advertise; people come to your door, offer you cash, and walk away with your item. Win, win, win.

Consignment and eBay—if you're the seller, it takes some time. If you have someone sell for you, they will get a percentage of the sale. I have found it more complicated than I have the energy to deal with, so I donate or use Craigslist. I have organizing customers who love selling on eBay. Again, know your limits, your style, and find the best-selling fit for you.

Antique dealer—ask a real estate agent or friends for a recommendation on a local dealer.

REWARD

Congratulations! You have completed a room or a portion of the room. You've recycled, dumped, and donated. Celebrate by doing something new with your freshly acquired space. Go have coffee. Buy yourself some flowers. Invite a friend over for dinner, and show off your fresh space.

REVISIT

If you've set aside any items labeled "undecided" or decided you were not ready to give up yet, write a date on the calendar when you will get those boxes back out and look at them again.

After some time passes and the date appears on the calendar, crack open those remaining boxes and see how you feel about the contents. You may be ready to let go now. Maybe not. I revisit boxes in my attic at least once or twice a year, primarily keepsake items and business papers that have passed the required document retention time. Some keepsakes will continue to tug on your heart and "speak to you" just as loudly as they did the year before. That's okay. At least you're intentionally checking in and testing their tug on your heart.

You also need to revisit the areas you've organized after a period of time, simply to assess whether or not it's working for you. All organizing needs tweaking to arrive at the point of satisfaction, as you live with the changes for a period of time. Remember how everything changes, even you—so you need to keep checking in to keep tabs on what's working and what's not. Your organizing can change along with you and your household.

RETAIL

Now that you've purged your home of unnecessary stuff, you will find yourself shopping in the near future. After spending days sorting through the accumulation of months or years, you may feel hesitant to bring more things into the house. You can already see yourself years from now, plowing through another purge, and probably don't wish to repeat all the work just completed.

Here is a little exercise to inspire self-control when you find yourself in a two-for-one sale, visiting an auction, logging onto eBay, or having a conversation with your mother about inheriting the antique desk. Anything that comes into your house requires commitment from you. Imagine yourself standing at the altar, holding hands with "Such A. Deal," and imagine yourself saying . . .

 *The Shopper's Vow*

I, take you, (name of object), to be my new thing,
to have and to hold from this day forward.

In the presence of this cashier and these shoppers,
I commit a portion of my finite living space
to your storage, my limited energy and
finances to your necessary maintenance.

Wherever I go, you shall go.
And when your life is over,
I promise to provide you with proper disposal,
through resale, recycling, donation, or the dump.

Today, as I carry you across my threshold,
I cherish the promise of our new life together.

Okay, so maybe that was a little over-the-top, but I bet next time you'll catch yourself remembering the scene if you're considering a purchase that doesn't fit your culture!

Whether you realize it or not, you have made a commitment to your stuff. Based on your current value system, you have made conscious decisions about what comes into your home. Every time a material object crosses your threshold, you have made a commitment. Think of it this way: When you purchase an item, inherit an item, or accept a gift, you're committing to:

- store it appropriately, giving up a portion of finite space in your dwelling
- use it
- maintain it, repair it, and possibly replace it
- clean it and houseclean around it
- dispose of it appropriately when its life is over
- pay for it to be moved to your next home

Is it worth it?

Granted, your home is full of stuff. If you're reading this book, you have a current inventory of stuff in your house. So before you consider making your next purchase, think about the options in front of you regarding the current-stuff inventory.

Again, I recommend you ask the object, "What gives you the right to live in my house?" If the answer to either question is "nothing," it's time for the item to move on, or don't even bring it across your threshold in the first place. Why waste your money, time, energy, and space on an item that doesn't fit into your vision?

The best time to ask these questions is before you even purchase it or bring it home with you.

ROCKET SCIENCE . . . NOT

I can't tell you how many times I've looked up from an organizing project and thought to myself, *This process is amazing even though it's not rocket science.* I marvel at the personal freedom gained through the simple act of rounding up belongings and sorting them out. I love the feeling I get when I take yet another truckload of great stuff to a donation center and imagine the love and life those possessions will see when someone else takes them home.

There is no greater satisfaction for me than to know I've spent some time and effort with little to no expense, and improved my home by creating more space and more order, or added beauty and function. The reward is immeasurable when a customer or friend tells me her life was changed simply because she took hold of her possessions and life, and pointed them in the same direction.

You can make the changes you need. Help is available. Tools are in your grasp. Everything we've discussed is within your ability to comprehend, apprehend, and overcome.

So when do you
want to start?

"The unexamined life is
not worth living."

—Socrates

CONCLUSION

You may have noticed this book devotes only one chapter to how to organize. The proportion is fitting. The message isn't about the stuff. It's about your life.

Life is short. Some of your stuff will live longer than you will. Our lives are made up of moments we pass through, moments we drink in. Our hopes and dreams of what could have been become mixed with the lives we lead, and it all flies past us in the middle of soccer games, promotions, and baby showers.

I believe life is precious. I also believe we have a finite measure of life here on this physical planet. The life you're breathing now with your family, career, and geographic location, is going to last for a limited time.

And that's the point: to *live*. I don't want to spend all my time and energy taking care of stuff, organizing stuff, cleaning stuff, and moving stuff. I don't want to spend myself in frustration or held back by old issues, pain, or baggage. I am determined to have a productive life filled with experiences, rich relationships, meaningful work and play. How disappointing it would be to look back on my life and see years wasted in indecision or being tossed and blown by circumstances. I'd rather make good choices—intentional choices—that make a difference. My aim is to live a life guided by the things most important to me, leaving a legacy behind me.

We each are given countless opportunities in choosing our life's path. A great adventure lies ahead in knowing our hearts and following our dreams. Fully experiencing life and the world around us is one of our most precious gifts. The stunning reality is that even in our limited time to live, we have the power to leave a priceless legacy behind. Our lives matter. Our choices matter. The spending of our extraordinary selves counts and leaves a mark upon an infinite universe. I want to go out with my boots on, laughing hysterically, because it was such a great ride.

Remember how intentional life was defined as a math equation at the beginning of the book? Intentional Life = Vision + Decision.

$$IL = V + D$$

Intentional Life = Vision + Decision

I need to make one adjustment to our little equation . . .

$$\frac{IL = V + D}{T}$$

Intentional Life = Vision + Decision over Time

Establishing a culture doesn't happen overnight. Discovering Who-you-are-now doesn't happen in one day. Give yourself permission to grow and learn. Offer yourself grace for making spectacular mistakes and brilliant discoveries. Build a home that captures the heart you have and the life you love.

It *is* a great ride.

If it doesn't support you or what's important to you, *what's it doing in your house?*

ENDNOTES

CHAPTER 1

1.Erwin Raphael McManus, Chasing Daylight: Seize the Power of Every Moment (Nashville: Thomas Nelson, 2002), 36.

CHAPTER 2

1. Foster Cline and Jim Fay, Parenting with Love and Logic (Colorado Springs: Piñon Press, 1990). Press.

2. Randall Wallace, Braveheart, directed/performed by Mel Gibson (1995; Hollywood, CA: Paramount Pictures, 2000), DVD.

CHAPTER 3

1. Peter Lord, Soul Care (Grand Rapids, Baker Book House, 1990).

2. Abraham Lincoln, Gettysburg Address, November 1863.

CHAPTER 5

1. Lost in Translation, written and directed by Sofia Coppolo (2003; Universal City, CA: Focus Features/Universal Studios, 2004), DVD.

2. Jim Burnstein, Renaissance Man, directed by Penny Marshall (1994; Burbank, CA: Touchstone Pictures), film.

3. John Patrick Shanley, Moonstruck, directed by Norman Jewison (1994; Beverly Hills, CA: MGM), film.

4. Fran Walsh, et al., Lord of the Rings: The Two Towers, directed by Peter Jackson (2002; Los Angeles: New Line Cinema, 2003), VHS and DVD.

5. Christopher Nave, quoted in "Childhood Personality Traits Predict Adult Behavior: We Remain Recognizably the Same Person, Study Suggests," Science Daily, August 5, 2010, http://www.sciencedaily.com/releases/2010/08/100804151456.htm.

6. Sid Kirchheimer, "Personality Changes with Age," WebMD Daily Health News, May 12, 2003, http://www.connecticare.com/globalfiles/healthnews/article.asp?ID=0 91e9c5e8000fa69&Cat=0&Num=6.

7. Stephen R. Covey, First Things First Every Day: Daily Reflections—Because Where You're Headed Is More Important Than How Fast You Get There (New York: Simon and Schuster, 1997), February 12.

CHAPTER 6

1. Erwin Raphael McManus, An Unstoppable Force: Daring to Become the Church God Had in Mind (Loveland, CO: Group Publishing, 2001), 103.

2. Quoted in De Forest O'Dell, The History of Journalism Education in the United States (New York: Ams Press Inc., 1935), 107.

CHAPTER 7

1. Laurence J. Peter, Peter's Quotations: Ideas for Our Time (n.p.: William Morrow & Co., 1977), 125.

CHAPTER 11

1. From Covey, 7 Habits of Highly Successful People, Habit 2. See more on habit 2 at Stephen Covey's website at https://www.stephencovey.com/7habits/7habits-habit2.php.

2. Laura Ingalls Wilder, Little Town on the Prairie (1941; 1953; 1971; repr., New York, HarperCollins, 2008), 214.

CHAPTER 12

1. Harriet Schechter, Let Go of Clutter (New York: McGraw-Hill, 2001), 125.

2. Ibid., 122.

3. Ibid., 123.

4. Ibid., 124.

5. Ibid.

6. Linda Spangle, "The Wt. Loss Minute: Is Guilt an Emotion?" Weight Loss Café website, April 27, 2009, http://weightloss-forlife.com/ezine-009427_334.html.

RESOURCES SHERI RECOMMENDS

1. *Linda Spangle*

   Learn to recognize and manage emotional eating.
   www.weightlossjoy.com

2. *Dave Ramsey*

   Learn to manage your money, get out of debt,
   and build a financial future.
   www.daveramsey.com

3. *Laugh Your Way to a Better Marriage*
   Keep your marriage healthy through laughter and
   improved communication.
   www.laughyourway.com

4. *John Sheasby*
   Learn about grace, and how to know God as a son or
   daughter, not as a servant.
   www.liberatedliving.com

5. *Dr. Brené Brown*
   Learn how to embrace your own imperfection, and
   overcome shame.
   www.brenebrown.com

6. *Danny Silk, Family Life Pastor*
   Learn how to raise children in the balance of
   freedom and obedience, and keep your interpersonal
   relationships healthy.
   www.lovingonpurpose.com

Connect with Sheri at
www.sheribertolini.com